# Conflict in 19th Century Ireland

## THE DEVELOPMENT OF UNIONISM AND NATIONALISM

Dr Russell Rees

Colourpoint
Educational

# For Jean

© Dr Russell Rees and Colourpoint Books 2010

ISBN: 978 1 906578 55 8

This text is a revised edition of *Nationalism and Unionism in 19th Century Ireland*, R Rees, Colourpoint, 2001.
First impression

Layout and design: Colourpoint Books
Printed by: ColourBooks Ltd

**Colourpoint Books**
Colourpoint House
Jubilee Business Park
21 Jubilee Road
Newtownards
Co Down
BT23 4YH

Tel:  028 9182 6339
Fax: 028 9182 1900
E-mail: info@colourpoint.co.uk
Web-site: www.colourpointeducational.com

Dr Russell Rees is a graduate of the University of Ulster. He was awarded a PhD for his thesis on relations between Northern Ireland, the Irish Free State and Britain in the period 1945–51. Dr Rees is currently Head of History at Omagh Academy and has written a number of books about Irish history; these include *Ireland and British Politics* (1993), *Union to Partition, Ireland 1800–1921* (1995) and *Ireland 1905–25* (1998), all published by Colourpoint.

# Contents

# Copyright Information

## Picture Credits

*(by illustration number)*

From C Weygandt, *Irish Plays and Playwrights*, 1913   25
Library of Congress, Prints & Photographs Division:
  LC-USZ62-135374   28
  LC-DIG-cwpbh-03648   14
  LC-DIG-ggbain-0365   17
  LC-DIG-ggbain-0073   24
  LC-DIG-npcc-07656   27
  LC-DIG-pga-02521   12
From M Doheny, *The Felon's Track*, M H Gill & Son, Dublin, 1920   10
National Library of Ireland   3, 15, 16, 18
Perry-Castañeda Library, The University of Texas at Austin   5
Punch Cartoon   20, 21, 23
From T Ó Néill, *Fiontán Ó Leathlobhair*, 1962   8

# Acknowledgements

A number of individuals have provided valuable assistance in the completion of this project. My colleague, Audrey Hodge, took the time to read a draft of the manuscript, while another friend and colleague, Michael Murphy, was always on hand to offer support and advice. Once again, the staff at Colourpoint have undertaken their tasks in their usual quick and efficient manner. In particular, I would like to thank Rachel Irwin for her editorial support.

Over the years I have gained fresh insights into nineteenth century Irish History through my association with the Sixth Form pupils of Omagh Academy and through lectures delivered to A level students at a number of venues. For this I am grateful to Richard Parkinson (Somme Heritage Centre), Finbar Madden (St Columb's College Derry), Jim McBride (Foyle and Londonderry College), Helen Parks (Methodist College Belfast) and Prof Alan Sharp (University of Ulster).

My greatest debit is to my wife, Jean, who typed the entire manuscript and was a constant source of encouragement and support.

*Dr Russell Rees*

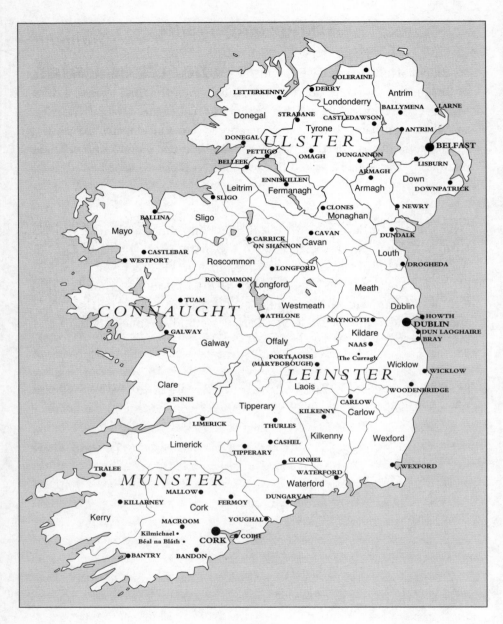

*Ireland*

*Chapter 1*
# The Act of Union

THE ACT OF UNION encompassed two identical measures passed in 1800 by the British and Irish Parliaments. It took effect from 1 January 1801 and joined Britain and Ireland together in the United Kingdom. The act abolished the Irish Parliament, which occupied the present Bank of Ireland building in Dublin's College Green. Thereafter, one hundred Irish MPs sat in the House of Commons at Westminster, while twenty-eight Irish peers and four Church of Ireland bishops took their seats in the House of Lords. The act also included interim arrangements to adjust trade tariffs between the two countries, and these were gradually phased out altogether, leading to the establishment of free trade from 1824. The impact made by these financial changes was negligible, and they merely accelerated the advance of an economic union between the two countries, which was already taking shape in the second half of the eighteenth century. Even politically, there was considerable continuity with the pre-Union era. While the removal of the Dublin Parliament provided an obvious break, the whole complex machinery of the Castle administration not only remained in place but was substantially increased over the course of the nineteenth century. Clearly, Ireland would not follow the Scottish example and become fully integrated into the United Kingdom system of government.

The chief architect of the Union, William Pitt, the Prime Minister, had indicated that the Union would allow Irish problems to be tackled in a more efficient and sympathetic manner. Ireland would, he argued, enjoy all the benefits that would automatically flow from her new relationship with Britain. Indeed, Pitt had been a consistent advocate of a legislative union between Britain and Ireland, believing that it offered the only really long-term solution to Ireland's difficulties. The Union, therefore, was not a knee-jerk reaction to the events of 1798, when a serious rebellion in Ireland had momentarily diverted British attention during the great turn-of-the-century conflict with revolutionary France. Instead, Pitt seized on the opportunity presented by the rebellion to bring forward his scheme for a Union. Still, Pitt's attempt to bring stability to Ireland was also dictated by wider imperial concerns. For the governing elite at Westminster the rebellion in 1798 had confirmed that Irishmen could no longer be left to manage their own affairs. Irish instability now threatened British security, and Pitt had little difficulty in persuading the House of Commons to support a new form of direct rule, though the lack of real attention given to Irish problems by the cabinet in London was to become a recurring theme during the course of the nineteenth century.

The events of 1798 had also concentrated the minds of Irish Protestants. Nearly 10,000 people had been killed during the rebellion, and to many onlookers in Ireland the violence had all the characteristics of a civil war. Pitt sought, therefore, to exploit this sudden feeling of Protestant vulnerability in order to garner support for his Union project among the country's decision-makers. Yet their simplistic view of the rebellion as a shocking example of Catholic disloyalty, and one that could be repeated, concealed the true nature of the insurrection. Ireland had witnessed a serious rebellion in 1798 when perhaps as many as 50,000, in places as far apart as Counties Antrim and Wexford, fought to turn Ireland into a democratic republic free from British influence. While all the participants could subscribe to this general aim, it was apparent that they had been motivated by a number of very different factors. The United Irishmen, as their name suggests, saw Presbyterians in the north join forces with Catholics in the south. This collaboration contributed to the complex mix of urban political radicalism, which had been influenced by recent revolutionary events in America and France, and serious agrarian unrest, based on the secret society tradition in rural Ireland, together with a strong conspiratorial element at the heart of the United Irish leadership. All of these combined to produce an insurrection in 1798. Crucially, the conspirators had colluded with revolutionary France and, though a small French invasion force had successfully landed in County Mayo, swift action by the British fleet prevented the main body of French troops from reaching Irish shores.

For Westminster, therefore, an immediate concern was the need to prevent a further invasion attempt. These events ensured that the long-term better government of Ireland was not the sole objective when Westminster embarked on its Union project. Fears of a fresh invasion attempt and the need to protect its Irish flank exerted a powerful influence on British thinking. Britain had been at war with France since 1793, and Pitt knew that the French could exploit further unrest in Ireland by launching an invasion, either to divert British attention away from the war on the continent or to provide a bridgehead for a subsequent invasion of the mainland. In these circumstances the Union was the surest way of returning Ireland to stability and reducing the prospect of another invasion attempt.

The occasion of the 1798 rebellion provided Pitt with the opportunity to press the case for a Union. In doing so Pitt repeatedly reminded members of the Protestant Ascendancy, the landowning elite which had dominated Irish society in the eighteenth century, that their survival depended on the security offered by the British state, something that could be more effectively delivered if the two countries were united under a single government. The 1798 rebellion had clearly demonstrated the vulnerability of the Ascendancy class in the face of a popular uprising and its dependence on British forces for protection. Indeed, the British had acted swiftly and decisively in suppressing the rebellion. An elaborate spy network had ensured that the revolutionary movement was kept under tight surveillance, and key leaders were already in custody when the insurrection began. An effective campaign of terror during 1797, led by the army, had already weakened the United Irish organisation in Ulster. Thereafter, a savage military response to the outbreak of revolutionary violence in 1798, followed by systematic and brutal repression, guaranteed a crushing victory for government forces. Significantly, during these engagements the Irish yeomanry, an almost exclusively Protestant force with a strong Orange Order influence, acquired a savage reputation for indiscipline and sectarian violence. Raised in 1796 to meet the twin threat of internal rebellion and foreign intervention, the yeomanry acted as the government's military spearhead in Ireland. Both during and after the rebellion members of the yeomanry were implicated in numerous murders and arson attacks on a large number of Catholic churches. By 1799, with its membership rising to 66,000, the yeomanry contributed to the growing impression that repression would become a key feature of British rule in Ireland.

As Chief Secretary for Ireland, Lord Castlereagh took responsibility for steering the Union legislation through the Irish Parliament. In his efforts to persuade the Protestant Ascendancy, whose members dominated the Parliament in Dublin, to back the idea of a legislative union, Castlereagh made effective use of the patronage system. New titles were created for a number of Irish MPs, while more were generously compensated in other ways, and this guaranteed a measure of support for the new initiative. However, more Irish MPs were convinced by Pitt's argument that only direct control from Westminster could restore firm government to Ireland and look after the long-term interests of the Ascendancy class. In the wake of the 1798 rebellion, this view was decisive in securing a majority for the Union in the Irish Parliament. Not surprisingly, those members of the Ascendancy who favoured a legislative union were primarily motivated by self-interest. Previously, the Irish Parliament had been successful in defending Protestant privileges, but a growing number of the Ascendancy class now believed that this task could be more effectively met by the Parliament in London which was, of course, familiar with the relevant religious arguments. Ironically, a majority of the educated Catholic middle class also favoured a legislative union, believing that it offered the best prospect for the amelioration of Catholic grievances. This had been the message that the British government had been transmitting, as it actively encouraged Catholics to believe that the Act of Union would be followed quickly by legislation which would finally concede Catholic emancipation. Pitt had intended that legislation granting Catholic emancipation would accompany the Act of Union, but he dropped this idea once it became clear that the introduction of such a controversial measure would create major difficulties in both Britain and Ireland. Still, Catholics were hopeful that their claims for just treatment would receive a more sympathetic hearing in the Westminster Parliament, and early progress on this issue was expected. Moreover, Catholic support for the Union was a significant factor in determining the measure's ultimate success.

In addition to the security aspect, Pitt also hoped that the Union would consolidate British control over Ireland and, simultaneously, would improve Anglo-Irish relations by removing the risk of a serious conflict between the Parliaments in London and Dublin. Friction between the two Parliaments was scarcely concealed, and the likelihood of a major constitutional clash had grown significantly in the second half of the eighteenth century. In this period two particular features influenced the development of Irish politics. Firstly, the Protestant Ascendancy had to confront the growth of Catholic power with the emergence of a small, educated Catholic middle class. Predominantly involved in business and trade, this emerging Catholic middle class had become increasingly important in Irish commercial life, and this contributed to the raising of political consciousness among its members. Not surprisingly, this growing political awareness soon found expression in opposition to the Penal Laws, a series of discriminatory measures directed against the Catholic population. Aimed at consolidating Protestant power following the Williamite victory in the 1690s, the Penal Laws imposed significant social, economic and political constraints on Catholics for most of the eighteenth century. While the impact of the Penal Laws was most keenly felt by the declining landowning class, the commercial middle class escaped the worst effects of the legislation and encountered few obstructions on their route to economic success. It was this Catholic middle class that led the struggle for the removal of Catholic grievances and, in the last quarter of the eighteenth century, a series of Catholic Relief Acts began the process of dismantling the Penal Laws. By 1793 Catholics, who met the franchise qualification, had won the right to vote and this opened the way to further political progress, even though they were still banned from holding certain public offices.

The second major development shaping Irish politics in this period was the growing hostility between the London and Dublin Parliaments. There had long been suspicion of England's intentions in Ireland among some members of the Ascendancy class, but this was to crystallise into a distinctive 'patriot' faction in the Irish Parliament in the latter part of the eighteenth century. The appearance of this patriot group was predictable. The superior attitude frequently adopted by the English in their dealings with Ireland was bitterly resented by a self-confident social and political elite, which assumed that it was, at the very least, the equal of the ruling class in England. In addition, it became increasingly apparent that Irish and English interests were often incompatible. Therefore, the patriot faction's initial political forays focused on the defence of Irish interests and the assertion of Irish rights. These factors contributed to a new awareness of Irishness and a growing spirit of independence among the patriot group and their supporters. The Protestant Ascendancy's brief dalliance with 'patriotism' marks the beginning of political nationalism in Ireland, and though it developed in a different form, as elitist Protestant nationalism gave way to popular Catholic nationalism in the nineteenth century, the central demand for Irish self-government remained constant. Another common strand was the tendency to express one's Irishness in a negative manner, and the anti-English rhetoric emanating from the patriot leaders set a pattern which influenced subsequent nationalists.

The clear aim of the patriots was to end Westminster interference in Irish affairs. Although they acknowledged that Ireland was a possession of the British Crown, the patriots claimed that Ireland was a separate kingdom which should be free to have its own laws made by its own Parliament. By the late 1770s, Henry Grattan, who had only been an MP since 1775, emerged as the leader of the patriot party, and he championed the cause of parliamentary independence, arguing that Ireland was an independent nation under a joint Crown. Of course, this nation was very narrowly defined. While it had a strong cultural and historical dimension, membership of this political nation was confined to that exclusive Protestant caste, or Anglican to be more precise, who were born in Ireland. In advocating legislative independence, these Protestant nationalists were demanding the restoration of Ireland's previous rights which, they claimed, had been gradually whittled down by the actions of the Westminster Parliament. What gave real impetus to the patriot struggle, and created the opportunity for the advancement of the patriot cause, was the conflict between England and her American colonies. Serious differences between the two led to the outbreak of war in 1775, and a series of disastrous military engagements for the British resulted in the loss of the colonies in 1782. The patriot faction in the Irish Parliament was quick to exploit the American conflict. Links between Ireland and America had been forged by large-scale emigration earlier in the century, and Grattan and his followers stressed the parallel between the Irish constitutional situation and the American challenge to British authority, while repeating their assertion that, unlike the colonies, Ireland was demanding nothing new, only the restoration of lost rights. Of course, the success of the American colonists served as a warning to the Westminster government in its dealings with Ireland and made English politicians more willing to listen to Irish grievances. The war with America also had dire economic consequences for Ireland. The Irish economy was already in a depressed state, but the trade restrictions caused by the war greatly exacerbated these difficulties, thereby adding urgency to the political demand for legislative independence.

What tipped the balance in the patriots' favour was the entry of France into the American war in June 1778 on the side of the colonists. Regular troops stationed in Ireland had already been dispatched across the Atlantic, and the French intervention opened up the possibility of an attack on an inadequately defended Irish coastline. To meet this French invasion threat, the Protestant gentry quickly established Volunteer corps throughout the country. Shortly after their formation the Volunteers numbered close to 40,000, with the rank and file drawn principally from well-to-do Protestants and serving under officers who were generally of landowning stock. Ostensibly, they provided a part-time military force to supplement the depleted regular army and to preserve law and order in the countryside, but they quickly acquired a political significance. By this stage the more militant patriots recognised the potential of an alliance with the Volunteers to press their claims for legislative independence. Although the patriots still constituted a minority in the Irish Parliament, the Volunteers provided them with a national organisation to promote their political aims, while acting as a powerful, and armed, extra-parliamentary force standing behind an increasingly confident patriot leadership. With Grattan and his followers now rallying public opinion throughout the country, the government in London could no longer ignore the situation in Ireland. Under pressure, it moved to relax commercial restrictions on Irish trade, but this only encouraged the patriots to seek further concessions. While a second attempt by Grattan to force legislative independence through the Irish Parliament in February 1782 was unsuccessful, it was apparent that the government could not hold out indefinitely. Both the content of the parliamentary debate and the recent activities of the Volunteers provided an indication of the momentum that the patriot cause had established.

The final piece in the jigsaw arrived with a change of government at Westminster in March 1782. In opposition, the Whigs had encouraged the Irish dissidents. Now in government, they signalled that the patriot demands could expect a sympathetic hearing, and Grattan wasted no time in moving a formal declaration of independence in April 1782. While Ireland was not granted 'legislative independence' in the strictest sense, the patriots had won significant political concessions. The shackles which had inhibited the Irish Parliament's room for manoeuvre were removed, but the change did not produce self-government as the Irish executive remained under Westminster control. In reality, the new constitutional arrangements made little impact on Irish society. The patriots were conservative by instinct, and internal squabbles soon undermined the unity of purpose so evident in the 'victory' of 1782. Yet 'Grattan's Parliament', as the years 1782–1800 became known, was of major symbolic importance. The concessions won from the British became a source of great pride and the period was marked by a welcome economic recovery. In addition, the parliament building in College Green became a symbol of national freedom. Moreover, the factors which had brought success to the patriots were not lost on later generations of nationalists. The mobilisation of popular support in Ireland, the fear of a French invasion, Britain's involvement in a major conflict and the collapse of a hostile government at Westminster each combined to advance the patriot cause. Of course, the decisive element in Grattan's triumph had been the extra-parliamentary pressure exerted by the paramilitary force of semi-political Volunteers.

The action of the thirteen American colonies in declaring their independence from Britain had been a major influence on Ireland. The American war breathed new life into Irish politics and a new political vocabulary emerged. Constitutions, rights, representation, independence and even revolution were now subjects for discussion among the politically conscious. Acutely aware of the constitutional inferiority of the Irish Parliament, the patriots seized the opportunity to attack British legislative interference. Although the last two decades of the eighteenth century have been described as a golden age for the Ascendancy class, Grattan's Parliament was not a success. In winning legislative independence and yet maintaining the British connection, Grattan and the patriots had achieved their purpose, but their use of this new freedom was disappointing. They rejected Volunteer demands for parliamentary reform, and they had neither the will nor the foresight to tackle the Catholic question. While the patriots regarded themselves as the Irish nation, this could not conceal the fact that eighty per cent of their fellow countrymen were Catholics whom the Irish Parliament decided should be kept in subordination. While Grattan personally wished to grant full political rights to Catholics, he was clearly in a minority, and the various measures of Catholic relief, notably the act of 1793, which gave the vote to wealthy Catholics, were imposed by Westminster against the determined opposition of the Irish Parliament. In effect, the patriots had won a Protestant Parliament for the Protestant nation, and a very narrowly defined Protestant nation at that. What they offered was a limited and exclusive form of nationalism, and this was reflected in the Irish Parliament's opposition to reform. However, in spite of these obvious deficiencies, the recovery of Grattan's Parliament became the motivation for every subsequent constitutional nationalist movement.

The 1798 rebellion and the subsequent Act of Union had combined to undermine Protestant nationalism. When challenged by the revolutionary forces of the United Irishmen, the weakness of the Irish Parliament was suddenly exposed. Moreover, the rebellion had highlighted the minority status of the Protestant Ascendancy and raised serious questions about its future security. Against this background, Irish MPs in Dublin struggled to produce a viable alternative and, therefore, accepted, albeit reluctantly, the British government's case for a Union. In time, it became clear that both the rebellion and the Union had deepened divisions within Ireland. Yet it would have been extremely difficult to predict developments following the implementation of the Union. The rise of popular Catholic nationalism, the decline of Presbyterian radicalism and the movement of nearly all Ascendancy opinion in favour of the Union were each, in their own way, surprising. While the development of some form of anti-Union sentiment was predictable, no one could be sure what pattern this would follow. Indeed, the picture at the beginning of the nineteenth century was complex. During the great public debate the Union enjoyed the support of both the Catholic hierarchy and a significant section of the Catholic middle class, but was vociferously opposed by a group of Catholic lawyers. On the other hand, the attitude of the recently formed Orange Order was unclear, with the leadership recommending a neutral stance on the question. And though the great wave of national feeling that swept the country in 1782 had, by this stage, clearly evaporated, many high-profile Ascendancy figures, including Grattan himself, remained opposed to the Union. Therefore, both Protestants and Catholics were divided on their attitude to the Union. What was recognised by those who framed the Union, however, was that if it were to work, there would have to be reconciliation both within Ireland itself and between Ireland and Britain. For this to happen, an early resolution of the Catholic question was essential.

## Chapter 2
# The Rise of
# Constitutional Nationalism

Although Lord Castlereagh, the Chief Secretary for Ireland, had acknowledged in cabinet that those who opposed the Union had numbers on their side, he was reassured by the fact that the propertied classes overwhelmingly supported the new constitutional arrangement. Crucially, Pitt was convinced that there was sufficient popular support for the measure in Ireland to make the Union viable. Of course, Protestant supporters of the Union, led by Lord Clare, successfully campaigned for the Union to be made on a Protestant basis. They demanded security against a future Catholic threat, and they were totally opposed to any new measure of Catholic emancipation which would have opened up those remaining public offices still closed to members of the Catholic religion following the various relief measures in the late eighteenth century. Indeed, many of these prominent supporters of the Union believed that such a concession would only encourage further rebellion, and their support for the Union was based on the assumption that direct rule from Westminster would make Catholic emancipation impossible. Where Catholics had comprised eighty per cent of the population in Ireland, they only made up twenty per cent of the United Kingdom population after the Union, and this left Protestant supporters of the Union confident that Catholic pressure for emancipation could be rebuffed. It also quickly became apparent that, in spite of the Union, Ireland would not be governed on the same basis as Britain. A separate executive, complete with many of the trappings of Ascendancy rule, remained in Dublin, and the Union quickly became identified with the defence of Protestant privilege in Ireland.

Irish Catholics, meanwhile, were disappointed that the Act of Union had not been accompanied by a simultaneous measure granting emancipation, but they fully expected such legislation to be enacted in the very near future. Moreover, this appeared to coincide with Pitt's thinking. The Prime Minister had originally intended to extend Catholic rights within the terms of the Union but then opted for a more cautious approach, fearing that the entire Union project might be jeopardised. Still, Pitt retained his support for emancipation and in the autumn of 1800 he returned to the issue, attempting to secure the backing of his cabinet before approaching the King. Unfortunately for the Prime Minister, and for the Irish Catholics, Pitt's strategy backfired. Some of his cabinet colleagues were unsettled by what they regarded as Pitt's use of devious tactics, but the principal reason for his failure was the King's continued opposition to the measure. Pitt had hoped to present George III with a *fait accompli*, arguing that emancipation was central to the government's Irish policy. The King, however, remained resolute in his religious objections to emancipation, and he was determined to assert royal power, sensing that Pitt had an ulterior motive in seeking to undermine the monarch's constitutional authority. In the end, Pitt accepted the King's position and, in his desire to remain in office, pledged to resist Catholic emancipation in deference to the monarch. This put the Protestant elite in Ireland at ease, as it was widely assumed that emancipation would no longer be considered while George III remained on the throne. Consequently, 1801 can be viewed as a missed opportunity, because an early resolution of the Catholic question would have given the Union a much firmer foundation. Pitt had believed that emancipation would be necessary to make the Union work, and it can be assumed that both the Catholic hierarchy and the small Catholic landowning class would have had good reason to support the state had emancipation been carried at this early juncture. In addition, the growing feeling of disenchantment, which in time would grow into a sense of betrayal because of Westminster's failure to deliver emancipation, was to be felt most keenly by the emerging Catholic middle class in Ireland. It was this group that launched a new style of nationalism, which emerged to challenge the status quo after 1800.

With mainstream political leaders at Westminster reluctant to embrace emancipation, the Catholic cause after the Union was taken up by a growing number of liberal Protestant MPs. The greatest champion of emancipation in this period was Henry Grattan, who had won a Yorkshire seat in 1805 but represented a Dublin constituency from 1806 until his death in 1820. Grattan argued that it was time to end the religious discrimination that belonged to a bygone age, and he claimed to speak with the full backing of Irish Catholics. After Grattan, the emancipation cause in Parliament was advanced by William Conyngham Plunket, the Enniskillen-born MP for Trinity College, Dublin, whose 1822 Catholic Relief Bill was passed by the House of Commons but rejected by the Lords. Plunket believed that emancipation would help to remove divisions in Irish society and restore political stability and peace to an increasingly restless Irish countryside. These liberal Protestant exponents of emancipation had some grounds for believing that the new King, George IV, was more favourable to Catholic relief than his father, but such optimism proved unfounded. More than twenty years after the Union, therefore, the opposition of the monarchy, the House of Lords and key members of the governing classes seemed as entrenched as ever.

In Ireland, meanwhile, Catholics struggled to present a united front on the crucial question of emancipation. Of course, they had expected emancipation to be pushed through Parliament in the wake of the Union, but their response was surprisingly muted when this failed to materialise. The primary reason for the failure of Irish Catholics to adopt a clear strategy aimed at winning emancipation centred on divisions within their ranks. While the representatives of the remaining Catholic gentry insisted on a cautious approach, anxious to promote cordial relations with the British government, a growing number of middle class Catholics favoured more assertive agitation, demanding concessions for Catholics and an end to injustice. This tension was mirrored in the ranks of the Catholic Committee, the pressure group that directed the campaign for emancipation in the early years of the nineteenth century. Matters really came to a head with the veto controversy in 1808. As the prospects for emancipation became a little brighter, the conservative wing of the committee sought to make the measure more palatable to the authorities at Westminster by indicating their support for a proposal to give the British state the power of veto in the appointment of Catholic bishops. In the bitter exchanges that followed, the middle class opponents of the veto successfully argued that such a concession would undermine Catholic freedom, and they emphatically rejected any move designed to give the government control over clerical appointments. Although the veto controversy resulted in a victory for the more radical section within the Irish Catholic leadership, divisions and personality clashes continued to plague the campaign for emancipation.

By 1810, however, the more progressive, bourgeois element on the Catholic Committee was clearly in the ascendant, and one of their number, Daniel O'Connell, had emerged as the leading spokesman for this group. O'Connell was born into a Catholic landowning family in County Kerry and educated in France before returning to Ireland to practise as a lawyer. Almost immediately, he was drawn to politics, and in his first public speech in 1800 he famously condemned the Union. Later dubbed the 'Liberator' for his contribution to the winning of Catholic emancipation, O'Connell became the dominant figure in Catholic politics in the first half of the nineteenth century. If Grattan was the first leader of constitutional nationalism in Ireland, it was his successor, O'Connell, who gave it a mass following, though this was to be some time in coming. Grattan and other liberal Protestants continued to press the emancipation case in the House of Commons, but there was frequent disagreement with, and among, Irish Catholics on the exact nature of the concessions that they would have to make in return for emancipation. This continued to stifle real progress.

The veto controversy had driven a wedge between English and Irish Catholics. While English Catholics, and indeed many of Ireland's bishops, had no objection to the government in London having some measure of control over the Catholic Church, O'Connell refused to yield on the principle of unqualified emancipation. His was the crucial voice in persuading Catholic opinion in Ireland to demand full Catholic emancipation with no strings attached. Yet a minority on the Catholic Committee continued to oppose such a bold strategy, and Catholic gentry leaders, such as Lord Fingall, shared the views of Plunket and other liberal Protestant supporters of emancipation who regarded O'Connell as an extremist. While this absence of unity made it impossible to mount a sustained drive for emancipation, O'Connell also recognised that a further reason for the failure to make headway with the Catholic cause was due to the determined opposition of Sir Robert Peel. One of the great political figures of the nineteenth century, Peel was Chief Secretary for Ireland from 1812–18. On taking office, Peel moved quickly to clarify Dublin Castle's outright opposition to emancipation, and he proved a brilliant defender of the status quo when the issue of Catholic relief came before the House of Commons.

Frustrated by Peel's rebuttals and seething at the divisions among the Irish Catholic leadership, O'Connell realised that a new approach was essential if Catholics were to be granted full political rights. His strategy was to mobilise the Catholic masses in support of emancipation. Previously, of course, Catholic agitation had been very narrowly based, something which was partly attributable to the fact that only the Catholic gentry and middle class would benefit directly from an emancipation victory. When O'Connell launched a new Catholic Association in 1823, its leadership consisted of the same elements that had dominated previous emancipation campaigns. However, of crucial importance at this point was O'Connell's intention to give the association a wider appeal. He ensured that it would campaign not just solely for emancipation but would seek the redress of Catholic grievances in general. Still, the mobilisation of the masses did not immediately follow the establishment of the new movement. What transformed the situation was the introduction of the 'Catholic rent' in 1824, which allowed new members to become 'associates' of the Catholic Association for the sum of *one penny per month. This attracted huge numbers and produced the first mass movement in Irish politics. Money was collected outside church doors on Sundays, under the watchful eye of parish priests, before being forwarded to the movement's Dublin headquarters. Within a year of its launch, £20,000 had been transferred to the Catholic Association's coffers. This dramatic development had two consequences. Firstly, it gave the Catholic clergy an important political role, which cemented the relationship between nationalism and Catholicism. Secondly, it allowed the Catholic masses to experience direct participation in a great national political struggle.

O'Connell's charismatic leadership and reputation as a man of the people were other vital ingredients in the spectacular growth of the Catholic political nation. His record was impressive. O'Connell had opposed the Union from the outset, and he had consistently identified both politically and in his legal work, with the Catholic cause and the protection of Catholic interests. His eagerness to defend the Irish people against the might of the Protestant establishment won him favour, and he successfully exploited the latent anti-English feeling existing among the Catholic masses. Previously, rural discontent had been channelled into the myriad of secret societies, which continued to play a pivotal role in the Irish countryside. More prominent in periods of economic distress, these secret societies, which often exhibited sectarian undertones, were primarily concerned with specific local issues such as rents, tithes and evictions, but they also provided

* meant that poor catholics could join and have their say.

21

a forum for the expression of political grievances. Moreover, resistance to authority was the common element in all secret societies, and this was reflected among large sections of the population. Beyond the clandestine activity of the secret societies, the Catholic middle classes had recently acquired great wealth and they dominated Catholic politics. Acutely aware of the power of Catholic numbers in Ireland, this bourgeois vanguard was becoming increasingly impatient with the system of government at all levels in Ireland. Only a handful of the public offices available to Catholics before emancipation had been filled by Catholics, and the arrangements for the administration of the counties caused particular anger. The Grand Juries, which administered the counties, were the fiefdoms of the Protestant gentry, and they became an obvious target for Catholic nationalism in the early decades of the nineteenth century. Indeed, patronage, which operated for the almost exclusive benefit of the Protestant elite, continued to oil the political system in Ireland for many years after the Union.

In the twenty years following the 1798 rebellion the Catholic peasantry also underwent a sharp rise in political consciousness. This happened for a number of reasons. The rebellion itself provided a reference point for disgruntled peasants, and O'Connell, while denouncing violence, frequently exploited the memory of the rebellion in rallying support for the Catholic cause. Increased social interaction among the peasantry at all kinds of gatherings, such as fairs, funerals and sporting events, also contributed to this growing political consciousness, and the peasantry quickly became familiar with the concept of concerted action. A rise in sectarian tension was another development that heightened political awareness. One reason for this was a reaction to the impact of Protestant evangelism, which was a feature of the years immediately after the Union, but reached a peak in the early 1820s. This direct threat to the Catholic Church partly explains the institution's willingness to become involved in a high profile political campaign under O'Connell's leadership. Furthermore, O'Connell deliberately broadened his campaign, allowing the drive for emancipation to be complemented by a desire to address Catholic grievances in general. Thus, every problem that affected the Catholic masses was politicised, and this translated into huge popular support for the Catholic Association in the 1820s. The most significant factor as far as rural Ireland was concerned, however, was the impact made by the network of secret societies in the Irish countryside. While contemporary Europe demonstrated that a rural population was particularly difficult to politicise, these secret societies in Ireland advanced the process of politicisation and provided experience in directing discontent.

Another significant factor in the development of a popular nationalist movement was the recent expansion of the Catholic Church. Seminaries in Ireland were opened and then reorganised to keep pace with the growing demand for clergy, and many of the new trainees were sons of well-to-do tenant farmers. This tended to produce a priesthood which was more in touch with its flock and was, accordingly, more attuned to political developments taking place in the local parishes. Consequently, only in early nineteenth century Ireland did the Catholic Church participate in a great popular reform movement. Elsewhere in Europe the church invariably attached itself to the forces attacking liberalism. Yet this did not mean that the Catholic Church took charge of the popular movement in Ireland. Leadership was firmly in the hands of O'Connell and his closest colleagues in the Catholic Association, but they recognised the value of collaboration with a sympathetic clergy who brought with them the organisational benefits of the Catholic Church. While O'Connell generally welcomed liberal Protestant support for emancipation, he was adamant that Catholicism should be the central feature of an emerging Irish nationality. From the early years of the nineteenth century, moreover, it was clear that religion had become a defining characteristic of popular political activity in Ireland. Naturally, the shift of Presbyterians to a more pro-Union stance was a significant factor in promoting the merger of Catholicism and nationalism, though the strengthening of Catholic consciousness had a greater impact. The growing wealth and influence of the Catholic bourgeoisie and the rise in political consciousness among Catholics across the social spectrum were key elements in this development. In addition, the Catholic Church identified with O'Connell's determination to tackle Catholic grievances and played its part in spreading national consciousness. Among the clergy's chief concerns was a desire to provide education for the children of the peasantry. This was a crucial factor in securing the active participation of the lower clergy in the campaign for emancipation. There was a widespread assumption among the priesthood that contributions to the Catholic rent would eventually filter back to the individual parishes, as it was anticipated that the money would be used to build schools or repair church buildings.

Of course, O'Connellism was a new political phenomenon. Although O'Connell can be described as the heir of Grattan, in the sense that he saw no contradiction between promoting Irish nationalism while remaining loyal to the Crown, his movement was much more dependent on popular support. Catholic emancipation became an issue of great symbolic importance, and the engagement of the masses transformed the campaign into a moral crusade. Yet this was never truly national in character, because the bedrock of support for O'Connellism was firmly based in Leinster and Munster. In both of these provinces there was huge expectation among the lower orders of the benefits for the entire Catholic population which would immediately follow emancipation. In the west, on the other hand, where poverty was endemic, the peasantry was generally too preoccupied with more mundane matters to have either the time or the will to indulge in politics. In the north, moreover, where there was the obvious problem associated with Protestant numbers, O'Connell struggled to win support for the emancipation cause.

In leading this agitation, O'Connell exploited the profound sense of injustice that had always existed among Catholics but had become more acute since the Union. This injustice had social, economic and political origins, and the perception was that the Union had exacerbated the problems facing Catholics. Moreover, the memory of the savage response of government forces to the 1798 rebellion was lodged in the Irish psyche. The sectarian backlash conducted by the Protestant yeomanry, under the auspices of the state, became a primary focus in the O'Connellite analysis of the rebellion more than twenty years later. Although O'Connell himself had taken the United Irish oath in the 1790s, he subsequently rejected violent nationalism. He was, however, astute enough to recognise the benefits of sharing a political platform with '98 veterans. Indeed, his speeches at these great public gatherings were frequently uncompromising and were regularly punctuated by violent language, which heaped abuse both on the British government and on the Ascendancy class in Ireland. Undoubtedly, this contributed to the growth of sectarian feeling, which had risen sharply in the first two decades of the nineteenth century. This also enabled O'Connell to castigate the Union itself which, he claimed, had been made on a Protestant basis and was directly responsible for many of the Catholic peasantry's grievances.

A temporary setback for the campaign occurred in 1825 when a group

KAT

of radical MPs at Westminster proposed a new Catholic Relief Bill, with certain safeguards designed to reassure Protestants. O'Connell's support for the measure drew sharp criticism from his more radical followers in Ireland, and further embarrassment was caused when the bill was defeated in the House of Lords. An angry O'Connell returned to Ireland in the summer of 1825 determined to renew the agitation, but it was at this point that the government moved to crush O'Connellism, which, by this stage, was regarded as a dangerous popular movement. The Catholic Association was suppressed, though O'Connell moved quickly to relaunch it as the New Catholic Association, and the campaign intensified. Attempts were also made to prosecute O'Connell for incitement to rebellion, but there was insufficient evidence and the charges were dropped. More aggressive than before, O'Connell now benefited from the assistance of his key followers. Richard Lalor Sheil, another lawyer who would become a prominent MP, had been an early opponent of O'Connell's tactics, but, by 1823, they had joined forces. Thereafter, Sheil became a powerful and effective advocate of emancipation, playing a prominent role in the mobilisation of the Catholic masses, and his alliance with O'Connell became crucial to the development of a successful organisation.

More importantly, Thomas Wyse, a prominent Catholic merchant, persuaded O'Connell that political progress could be made by utilising those enfranchised Catholics, the forty-shilling freeholders who had been given the vote in 1793, in the 1826 general election. Key constituencies were targeted and, much to O'Connell's surprise, it became clear that Catholic voters could defy instructions from their landlords and vote for the candidate of their choice, usually sympathetic liberal Protestants who backed emancipation. In these years before the secret ballot, the threat of eviction was usually sufficient to pull potentially independently-minded voters into line, but, from 1826, landlords had difficulty in countering concerted action by their tenants. This new development was famously highlighted in the Waterford constituency, where the pro-emancipation candidate, Henry Villiers Stuart, defeated the all-powerful Beresford family's candidate. Credit for this stunning success in Waterford, which ultimately paved the way for O'Connell's own triumph in Clare, was due to the initiative of local activists. Directed by Waterford-born Wyse, these men established a network of local branches to organise support in the county. Liberal Protestant support was sought and money was used to run a popular campaign. The key to success in Waterford, however, was the backing of the local clergy. Their earlier involvement in the collection of the Catholic rent had cemented their growing political authority, and their enthusiastic participation in the campaign proved to be the decisive factor in freeing the forty-shilling freeholders from landlord control.

The demonstration of Catholic electoral power in 1826 sent shockwaves through both the British government and the Protestant establishment in Ireland. It also surprised O'Connell who had been slow to see the potential of these Catholic voters. A change of government in 1827 promised an early resolution of the emancipation issue, but the sudden death of the new Prime Minister, George Canning, and the quick resignation of his equally sympathetic successor, Viscount Goderich, threw everything back into the melting pot. The new government was led by the Duke of Wellington, and both he and the experienced Home Secretary, Sir Robert Peel, or 'Orange' Peel as he was described by O'Connell, were assumed to be implacable opponents of emancipation, though Peel, as O'Connell's movement gained momentum, had privately acknowledged that the extension of Catholic rights was inevitable. At the same time, O'Connell renewed the emancipation agitation in Ireland and, in the early part of 1828, a series of impressive demonstrations of popular support took place throughout the country. Money was again pouring in from the Catholic rent, and it seemed that O'Connell was set on a collision course with the Westminster government. Matters came to a head that summer when a by-election was held in County Clare. The by-election was called following the appointment of William Vesey Fitzgerald, one of the MPs for Clare, to the cabinet as President of the Board of Trade. Following the convention of the day, any MP appointed to the cabinet had to resign his parliamentary seat in order to seek re-election. Although Vesey Fitzgerald was a very popular landowner who had been a firm supporter of emancipation, the Catholic Association was determined to oppose any parliamentary candidate who supported the Wellington-Peel administration. Only when a suitable candidate could not be found, did O'Connell allow his own name to go forward as Vesey Fitzgerald's opponent. While the existing oaths of supremacy and abjuration prevented O'Connell taking his seat if elected, there was nothing in the law to stop him contesting the seat, and so the scene was set for a dramatic by-election contest in July 1828.

The Clare by-election was a defining moment in the development of constitutional nationalism, and Peel certainly viewed it as a turning point in the campaign for emancipation. Amid scenes of unparalleled popular excitement, O'Connell's full oratorical powers were unleashed. He lambasted his opponent, tore into the Wellington-Peel government and presented himself as the defender of the Catholic people. Significantly, the Catholic clergy, particularly younger priests, were very prominent in the Clare contest, frequently addressing their flocks in Irish and urging them to defy their landlords by voting for the Liberator. Not surprisingly, in view of the tension surrounding the event, O'Connell himself resorted to sectarian rhetoric in some of his pronouncements. At the end of a dramatic and highly-charged campaign he was declared the victor by 2,057 votes to 982 votes. O'Connell's victory presented the Westminster government with a clear challenge. The prospect of the Clare result being repeated all over Catholic Ireland was one thing, but the possibility of Catholic agitation spilling over into serious violence, if the Conservative government continued to resist emancipation, was another. Sectarian bitterness was already on the increase with the formation, in August 1828, of the Brunswick Clubs. These were militant and aggressive Protestant societies, established to replace the Orange Order, which had recently been suppressed by the authorities. From the outset, these Brunswick Clubs warned that they were prepared to use force, if necessary, to prevent emancipation.

In reality, therefore, it was this new fear of civil disorder that determined the government's thinking, and a Catholic Emancipation Bill was introduced in February 1829. Despite some last ditch attempts to delay the inevitable, the King reluctantly gave the bill the royal assent on 13 April 1829. O'Connell had won a great victory, though the government attempted to check the power of O'Connellism by raising the franchise qualification from a forty-shilling freehold to a £10 freehold. Wellington had decided that it would be necessary for O'Connell to sacrifice the forty-shilling freeholders, as this allowed the Prime Minister to deflect opposition by claiming that his measure also strengthened the position of the responsible, propertied classes. This dramatically reduced the number of Catholic voters but, in the celebrations that followed, this new restriction was largely ignored. The Catholic political nation was jubilant and, delighted with its victory, the Catholic Association dissolved itself. Not surprisingly, the successful tactics used to prise this concession from the British government would not be forgotten. It was apparent, moreover, that the manner of the victory in 1829 had given constitutional nationalism very firm foundations.

The Emancipation Act opened up nearly every public office to Catholics, and a new oath of allegiance replaced the previously unacceptable expressions of loyalty. The main beneficiaries were members of the Catholic middle class. From 1829, some of them could sit in Parliament, while others gradually squeezed into the public positions now open to them. For the peasantry, the foot soldiers of the agitation, however, there was no material gain. It was anticipated that general improvements would follow emancipation, but, in reality, the victory of 1829 only raised Catholic expectations, which could not be met, and this was to have an important bearing on the future development of Irish nationalism. Yet the peasantry's participation in the great triumph undoubtedly gave them a new self-respect and, crucially, they became more aware both of their rights and of their numerical strength. In harnessing the masses O'Connell gave expression to these rights, and he recognised that the force of public opinion could be channelled to influence governments, even hostile Conservative ones. Thus, the agitation for emancipation became a great moral crusade, as the government was increasingly challenged by majority opinion in Ireland. Of course, in mobilising the peasantry, O'Connell, true to his liberal principles, was careful to ensure that the movement remained constitutional. Still, there was always the possibility of widespread civil disorder if concessions were not granted, and O'Connell's frequently militant rhetoric only reinforced this potential threat. In the end, this was to prove a decisive factor for the Wellington government, as it weighed up the risk of continued resistance to Catholic demands.

Although O'Connell consistently sought Protestant support during the campaign for emancipation, his oratory frequently aroused sectarian feeling. Earlier, in July 1826, he had declared that the Catholic people constituted the Irish nation and, while welcoming Protestant support, O'Connell stressed that Catholics would bear the real burden in the forthcoming struggle for justice. Much of his success was due to the special bond that he established with the Catholic masses who regarded him as one of their own. It would be wrong, however, to attribute undue blame to O'Connell for the growth of sectarian feeling in nineteenth-century Ireland. He led a mass movement which sought to redress a major Catholic grievance, and he relied on local parish priests to undertake much of the organisation at grass roots level. Naturally, this strengthened the relationship between

Catholicism and nationalism, but one consequence of this development was the creation of a major obstacle for subsequent leaders of nationalism who wanted to appeal across the sectarian divide. Previously, O'Connell had assumed that a political alliance with Irish Protestant liberals would yield success, but he gradually came to see the potential of Catholic electoral support and understood the advantages of exploiting the powerful sense of injustice felt among Catholics at every rung on the social ladder.

One lesson to be drawn from the emancipation victory was that it had been a triumph for Catholic self-reliance. For nationalists to win concessions, they had to confront the Westminster government directly, though such a course of action had to be buttressed by powerful agitation in Ireland. In the process, both the government and the Irish Protestant minority were suddenly made aware of the political power of the masses. In particular, the unprecedented scale of the agitation alarmed the Protestant Ascendancy, and it became clear that the Union offered their only means of protection from the growing Catholic threat. Yet this should not obscure the fact that O'Connell had involved the masses in constitutional politics and, ultimately, their victory was won in Parliament. In this sense he became the prototype leader for nineteenth-century popular political movements. His secret was his success in balancing radical and conservative support. O'Connell literally led from the front, closely identifying with his people and highlighting Catholic grievances in exuberant, strident public addresses. At the same time, his own conservative instincts helped him to retain the support of a cautious Catholic gentry and wealthy bourgeoisie, which was also vital in his campaign for emancipation. Thus, O'Connell had laid very firm foundations for constitutional nationalism, and it was this form of moderate, democratic nationalism that proved to be the dominant strain in nineteenth-century Ireland. Like Grattan's earlier achievement of legislative independence, however, Catholic emancipation was of more symbolic importance than practical benefit. The great triumph of 1829 also raised expectations among the new Catholic political nation, which saw it as a crucial first step on the road to an overhaul of the entire economic and political system in Ireland. Clearly, O'Connell had demonstrated that constitutional politics could work: the question now was how would he build on this success?

There was an assumption that if the power of Catholic numbers could deliver emancipation, then the masses could be mobilised to win further concessions, including the repeal of the Union. Here O'Connell had to perform another balancing act. While many of his supporters looked forward to radical social and economic reform, he himself was very conservative in his attitude to structural changes in Irish society. Rather, O'Connell saw improvement based on the attainment of an end to Protestant privilege and what he described as 'justice for Ireland', though precisely what this meant he chose not to define. Significantly, in spite of his outstanding qualities, O'Connell knew that his emancipation triumph would only guarantee popular support in the short-term and that definite progress on the equality issue was required if he were to retain this support. Expectations had, moreover, been raised by the success of the emancipation campaign. A highly politicised peasantry, acutely aware of the power of collective action, anticipated further success after 1829. Their primary concern, however, was the redress of Catholic grievances, and this confined Irish nationalism within fairly rigid sectarian parameters. One consequence of this, and the Protestant and Orange reaction, was the further sectarianisation of Irish politics, a development that clearly gathered pace in the 1820s. In developing this powerful Catholic nationalism, O'Connell and his lieutenants had also placed the church and its clergy in a position of real influence, though the key voices among the leadership in the country belonged to the wealthy Catholic bourgeoisie, who were most anxious for social and political influence.

O'Connell had always maintained that his great goal in political life was the repeal of the Act of Union. Accordingly, he founded the Society for the Repeal of the Union in 1830, and it was assumed that a repetition of the emancipation tactics would follow. Yet the two issues were entirely different. Emancipation had enjoyed considerable support in Britain, particularly among Whig MPs, and liberal Protestants in Ireland had endorsed the measure. The drive for repeal, however, aroused fears and suspicions about O'Connell's ultimate intentions, and the external support, which the emancipation campaign had enjoyed, was to be replaced by outright opposition to repeal. Furthermore, the agitation for repeal could neither generate the same support among O'Connell's middle class followers nor spark the same level of interest among the Catholic hierarchy. O'Connell was astute enough to recognise these obstacles and, though money again poured in, he took a cautious line on the repeal issue in this early phase. Indeed, even when the repeal agitation reached a crescendo in the early 1840s, O'Connell consistently refused to spell out precisely what he meant by repeal, a ploy that subsequent Irish nationalist leaders repeated in the Home Rule era. Most likely, repeal would have been based on the restoration of the legislative independence secured by Grattan, but a clear definition was unnecessary and probably would have been counter-productive. Instead, repeal became a rallying cry for O'Connell's nationalist supporters and was presented, as Home Rule would be later in the century, as a cure for all of Ireland's political and economic ills. Equally significant, however, was his measured use of the repeal issue as a lever to squeeze reforms out of a frequently unenthusiastic Westminster government. Therefore, O'Connell was prepared to alter his approach depending on the prevailing circumstances in Britain and Ireland.

When prospects looked brighter, as they did in November 1830 with the return of the Whigs to power, O'Connell would don his parliamentary hat and press the case for reform at Westminster. Although he never lost his fundamental belief in repeal, O'Connell was pragmatic enough to appreciate the value of achievable, incremental gains, which he could present to his followers as progress in his quest to bring justice to Ireland. Only when this reform avenue was firmly closed, did O'Connell virtually abandon Westminster and commit himself exclusively and unequivocally to repeal agitation in Ireland. However, during the 1830s, a decade of Whig domination, O'Connell concentrated on parliamentary activity, as he pushed for reform. Another factor influencing his decision to adopt a gradualist approach was the level of strife over large parts of rural Ireland in the early 1830s. To some extent he was responsible for this new wave of agrarian unrest, as his successful emancipation campaign had encouraged the belief that the redress of particular economic grievances was imminent. Furthermore, O'Connell had inadvertently demonstrated that direct action could resolve particular problems. In this instance rural discontent focused on the tithe, a tax paid by certain tenant farmers to support the established church, the Church of Ireland. The fact that most of those who were paying for the upkeep of the Church of Ireland were not members of this alien church only added to the sense of injustice felt by Catholics. Anti-tithe protests had been a feature of Irish rural society for some decades, but the level of disturbance generated by the agitation in 1830–33 led to government fears that the situation would quickly degenerate into chaos unless resolute action was taken. Tension was never far from the surface in rural Ireland, and any downturn in agriculture could provoke turmoil.

The Tithe War began in Leinster, though it quickly spread to other parts of the country, and violent clashes between the peasantry and the authorities became widespread. Agrarian secret societies expanded rapidly, and violence reached a peak in 1832 when 242 murders were committed. By 1833 there were more than twenty counties in which half or more of tithes owed were unpaid. The government responded with a series of coercive measures, and the yeomanry were used to assist the over-stretched police force in maintaining order. Violence increased when these government forces began to seize livestock and other goods in lieu of the unpaid tax. What made this agrarian campaign more effective was the level of support it enjoyed. Local clergy in rural areas frequently backed the campaign, and a number of senior clerics, such as John MacHale who would become Archbishop of Tuam in 1834, openly supported the abolition of tithes. More significantly, wealthier farmers, who routinely kept their distance from secret societies, were prominent in the anti-tithe protests. They had been hit by the extension of the tithes to grazing land in 1823, and these large farmers were particularly active in the Tithe War. While O'Connell's personal suspicion of secret societies meant that he remained aloof, his supporters often provided leadership at local level. In the end, relative peace only returned to the Irish countryside, when the government abandoned its policy of using police and soldiers to enforce payment of the tithes in June 1833.

This change of policy prevented a dangerous situation spiralling out of control. For O'Connell, who was very concerned at the level of rural disorder, the Whig government's apparent willingness to consider reform offered the possibility of progress. He was anxious that repeal agitation would not be confused with the anti-tithe protests, because, while there were political advantages to be gained from identifying with a popular cause, the threat to his political leadership from the activities of secret societies engaged in widespread intimidation and violence was obvious. As expected, O'Connell condemned government repression, but he was hopeful that Ireland's inclusion in the government's great scheme of parliamentary reform would allow him to increase his influence at Westminster. O'Connell was bitterly disappointed with the content of the 1832 Irish Reform Act. It gave Ireland only five additional seats, taking the total to 105, and it failed to return the franchise to the forty-shilling freeholders who had lost the vote in 1829. Denouncing Earl Grey's administration, O'Connell made repeal the dominant issue in the 1832 general election. Despite the restricted franchise, 39 MPs who pledged to support repeal were returned for Irish constituencies. Indeed, O'Connell had required candidates seeking his support in the general election to take a repeal pledge.

O'Connell now stood at the head of a party of 39 'Repealers', which included a generous sprinkling of his own family members, but it was soon apparent that the new House of Commons was no more sympathetic to the idea of repeal than the unreformed pre-1832 version. In addition, though repeal may have enjoyed great popular support in Ireland, most Irish MPs were absolutely opposed to any tampering with the Union. In these circumstances O'Connell opted for a policy of keeping repeal agitation ticking over in Ireland, while cooperating with Grey's new Whig administration in an attempt to secure specific reforms. This appeared the most effective way to use his political influence in London. The O'Connellite party was never the powerful instrument that Parnell had at his disposal in the 1880s, but this block of supporters gave him the opportunity to make a decisive intervention if the right parliamentary circumstances existed, and they did lay the foundations for the development of an independent Irish party at Westminster. In spite of the difficulties he encountered with Grey, O'Connell's overall strategy of using repeal to squeeze reform out of a reluctant government appeared to have some success. In 1833 the government at last recognised the need to look at the position of the Church of Ireland in the Irish Church Temporalities Act, which responded to, but did not settle, the tithe issue. Although O'Connell was dismayed by much of the detail in this new legislation, it did put down an important marker for the future disendowment of the Church of Ireland. Still, he had little to show for his policy of cooperation with the Whigs, and it appears to have been a combination of this sense of disillusionment and pressure from his more radical repeal followers which convinced him that he should abandon his cautious approach to repeal and take the issue to Parliament. Accordingly, in April 1834, O'Connell raised the repeal question in the House of Commons, and he must have been disappointed, but not surprised, at the scale of defeat, as the measure was rejected by 523 votes to 38. Clearly, unlike emancipation, there was no support whatsoever for repeal from any section of the two great parties at Westminster, and it must have been galling for O'Connell to be reminded that there was a clear majority of Irish MPs opposed to repeal.

O'Connell knew enough about political feeling at Westminster to expect a crushing defeat, but such a reverse probably suited his purpose at this stage. He had delayed bringing the repeal issue before Parliament until 1834, and it appears he had done so only reluctantly, following demands from his more headstrong supporters. O'Connell's immediate reaction to the rejection of repeal was to denounce the Union at a number of public meetings in Ireland, but he then chose to play down the repeal issue in the 1835 general election campaign. Instead, O'Connell made 'No Tories, No Tithes' his popular slogan for the duration of the campaign. Thereafter, he virtually abandoned the demand for repeal between 1835 and 1840. The scale of the anti-tithe agitation had highlighted serious problems in channelling popular discontent in Ireland during this period, and this encouraged O'Connell to seek closer cooperation with the Whig party. This development resulted in the Lichfield House compact, an informal alliance between the O'Connellites and the Whigs, which was agreed in March 1835. The immediate result was an agreement to combine their voting strength in the House of Commons in order to remove Peel's short-lived Tory administration. While there was no formal written agreement, the O'Connellites gave their full support to the new Whig government under Lord Melbourne in return for the promise of reform in a number of specified areas. Although he never abandoned his personal belief in the benefits of repeal, O'Connell's alliance with the Whigs highlighted another key tactic in the development of constitutional nationalism. Like later generations of constitutional nationalists, O'Connell had decided to test the Union in order to measure the benefits that might accrue to Catholic Ireland through cooperation with one of the two great parties at Westminster. If the Whig alliance did not produce the expected improvements, however, then O'Connell would be free to revive the repeal agitation in Ireland.

In terms of the legislative record, the results of the Lichfield House compact were extremely disappointing. In 1838 a Tithe Rent-charge Act was passed, which reduced tithe payments, wrote off the arrears that had accumulated since 1834 and altered the way in which the tithe was assessed and collected. While this did not abolish tithes, it did enough to ensure that the tithe issue ceased to be a source of popular discontent. In fact, the charges for tithes were now levied on the landlords rather than their tenants, and this proved sufficient to bring direct action to an end.

More significantly, perhaps, the Tithe Rent-charge Act removed the tithe-proctors, who were the focus of much of the opposition to this unfair tax. Another piece of legislation also focused on the question of poverty in Ireland. The 1838 Poor Relief (Ireland) Act extended the English poor law system to Ireland, but this English solution to an Irish problem did not prove effective. The population explosion in Ireland, and the consequent pressure on resources, had finally forced the government to consider some form of provision for the relief of poverty, but the inadequacy of the response was quickly exposed by the famine. The new poor law system was based on the workhouse, which was to be established in each of the 130 poor law districts and run by boards of guardians using money collected from local ratepayers. While a system which focused on the provision of employment through relief schemes during the summer period, the 'hungry months', when the previous year's potato harvest had been consumed, would have been more suitable to Irish conditions, no alternative scheme could have coped with the famine. O'Connell himself was dismayed by the poor law system which was established, and he actually voted against the measure, principally, it appears, because he thought that it would impose too heavy a financial burden on the country's property owners.

The final important element of Whig legislation dealt with municipal reform in Ireland. The 1840 Municipal Corporations Act also fell far short of Irish expectations, as many of the proposals made by O'Connell were ignored. The powers given to local councils under the act were not as extensive as those granted in England, and the local government franchise was confined to £10 householders, again more restrictive than on the mainland. While the reorganisation of local government in Ireland enabled O'Connell to become Lord Mayor of Dublin in 1841, the changes were disappointing, and the legislation only served to remind O'Connell that Ireland was denied equal treatment. In collaborating with the Whigs, O'Connell had focused on three major domestic themes on which he hoped that significant progress could be made. Although his strategy enjoyed the support of liberal Presbyterians in Ulster, O'Connell was surely disappointed by his failure to achieve major advances in parliamentary reform, municipal reform and the abolition of tithes. Clearly, neither the Whig alliance nor the Union itself was working.

Still, the alliance with the Whigs had produced positive results in other ways. The appointment of Thomas Drummond as Under-Secretary in 1835, a position which gave him control over the whole machinery of government based at Dublin Castle, was the key development of the decade for the governing of Ireland. With the support of the Lord Lieutenant, Lord Mulgrave, and the Chief Secretary for Ireland, Viscount Morpeth, Drummond began a root and branch overhaul of the Irish administration. Sympathetic to the plight of the peasantry, he scarcely hid his contempt for the Ascendancy class, believing that it was the attitude of the landowners which was responsible for most of the agrarian unrest in Ireland. Drummond also orchestrated an unrelenting campaign against the Orange Order, which opened the door to the selection of Catholic and liberal Protestant candidates for public appointments. Indeed, O'Connell was not slow in recommending deserving Catholics for many of these positions, and approximately one-third of the new executive's appointments went to Catholics. Meanwhile, much to O'Connell's delight, the Orange Order voluntarily dissolved itself in April 1836, fearing its suppression following a very critical parliamentary select committee report ordered by the Whig administration.

Of greater significance for ordinary Catholics, however, was Drummond's reform of policing which produced a more acceptable and impartial service. Catholics were encouraged to put themselves forward for recruitment to the new police force, and a number were successful in winning senior positions. Drummond also edged the justice system away from Ascendancy control, and a few Catholics actually became judges. These changes were, in reality, the fruits of the victory in 1829, but they had great symbolic importance, even though only a small section of the Catholic middle class was to benefit financially. Drummond's reforms also created a much better atmosphere in Ireland. This encouraged O'Connell to consider dropping his demand for repeal altogether, as it appeared that a more enlightened administration could deliver justice to Ireland. Still, this more effective working of the Union could not obscure the Whig government's poor legislative response to Irish needs. The strength and determination of the Conservative opposition, ably led by Peel, and the massed Tory ranks in the House of Lords both proved major obstacles, but there was always the suspicion that governments at Westminster, even sympathetic ones, had higher priorities than Ireland. Drummond had made a difference, but his death in 1840 was a serious blow to the O'Connellites. When the Melbourne government fell in the following year and the Conservatives took office under Peel, the pragmatic O'Connell was forced to review his strategy. The result was the renewal of the repeal agitation.

In fact, O'Connell was considering such a change in direction before Peel's accession to the premiership. In July 1840 he had launched the Loyal National Repeal Association, and it had been preceded by similar organisations in 1838 and 1839, developments which would suggest that O'Connell had become disillusioned with the outcome of the Whig alliance and was preparing for a return of the Tories. Perhaps surprisingly, the repeal agitation was slow to get off the ground, demonstrating that O'Connell could not turn on and off the agitation as he pleased. Further evidence of this apathy arrived in the general election of 1841, when only 18 Repealers were returned. With O'Connell devoting much of his time to his duties as Lord Mayor of Dublin in 1841–42, repeal looked to be an issue that would fail to fire the enthusiasm of the masses. Three developments transformed the situation. Significantly, Archbishop MacHale declared his support for repeal in 1842, and his initiative encouraged other members of the hierarchy and the lower clergy to participate in the new campaign. Secondly, a poor harvest in the same year caused economic distress, and this helped to fuel a new wave of popular discontent. At the same time, the situation was exploited by a group of radical, younger nationalists who had been attracted to the repeal movement. In October 1842 they produced the first edition of the *Nation*, a newspaper which they used to promote the campaign for repeal. The immediate impact of the *Nation*, which achieved circulation figures of 10,000 but enjoyed a readership of 250,000, principally through the use of the repeal reading rooms, quickly generated momentum for the repeal agitation. The key figures who founded the newspaper were Thomas Davis, a Protestant lawyer, Charles Gavan Duffy, a northern Catholic with experience in journalism, and John Blake Dillon, a Catholic from a well known Mayo business family and, like Davis, a graduate of Trinity College. These three were quickly joined by similar youthful, middle class intellectuals from both Catholic and Protestant backgrounds. They later became known as the 'Young Ireland' group.

Although serious differences later emerged between O'Connell and these Young Irelanders, they were, initially, fully behind O'Connell's repeal campaign. The *Nation*'s efforts to create a feeling of nationhood, and its general promotion of the nationalist cause, helped to rally the people, and O'Connell stood ready to spearhead the campaign which, after a few false starts, was now fully under way. Clearly, the main sphere of activity had now shifted from Westminster to Ireland. In January 1843, O'Connell declared that this would be 'repeal year', and the vast audiences that turned out to hear him reinforced his belief that the British government would capitulate, as it did in 1829, under the weight of popular opinion. Indeed, though not all of the Catholic hierarchy embraced repeal as they had emancipation, the two campaigns were remarkably similar. Repeal agitation was very much Catholic in character, and the lower clergy played a crucial organising role at local level. Again, money poured in, allowing O'Connell both to finance an impressive campaign of agitation and to meet his own considerable expenses. But the most abiding memory of the repeal agitation was the 'monster meeting', which attracted huge crowds anxious to hear O'Connell's brilliant denunciation of English misgovernment in Ireland. Between March and October 1843 there were approximately 40 such meetings, usually held on Sundays, drawing crowds frequently in excess of 100,000. The sites chosen for these demonstrations were famous historic locations, and this added to the excitement and sense of occasion generated by O'Connell's stirring oratory.

In terms of organisation and efficiency, and as a means of expressing popular opinion, these gatherings were phenomenal by contemporary European standards. O'Connell revelled in the display of patriotism evident in these monster meetings, and news of the campaign received full coverage in the *Nation*. Yet he refused, as before, to be drawn on precisely what he meant by repeal. The re-establishment of Grattan's Parliament was anticipated, but O'Connell preferred to rely on rhetoric and symbols rather than to explain how a new constitutional arrangement would work. His speeches during the summer of 1843 were full of defiant messages for the government at Westminster. There were frequent references to past wrongs done to Ireland and, occasionally, there were warnings of dire consequences if the government refused to give way. While these warnings were balanced by repeated declarations that the goal of repeal would be pursued by exclusively peaceful means, it was the possibility of serious violence that concentrated Peel's mind. Sometimes, the demonstrations appeared to be military in character, with large numbers marching in drill formation, while others on horseback, the 'repeal cavalry', were given prominent positions. Certainly, O'Connell wanted to raise the stakes in his desire to force a climbdown on the government's part, but it was also the case that most people in the vast crowds, whatever O'Connell's genuine personal assertions of loyalty to the Crown, were anti-English and welcomed the threatening language used by the 'Liberator', as he was known at this time. In June 1843 he issued his famous 'Mallow defiance', which rather ambiguously suggested that Irishmen might yet have to fight to win their freedom. Despite such provocative and intemperate language, there is no doubt that O'Connell himself was absolutely opposed to violence, and that he never envisaged reaching a stage which required the use of any kind of unconstitutional action on the part of the repeal movement. His real purpose was to use the monster meetings to apply huge moral pressure by demonstrating to the government that public opinion was clearly behind him. If, however, the government saw these demonstrations as a form of intimidation, O'Connell believed that it would only add to the desired effect.

In an attempt to recreate the successful formula which had brought success in 1829, O'Connell sought significant Protestant support for repeal. This was never forthcoming, because Protestant opinion was largely against repeal, though the Protestant element within the Young Ireland group was, of course, an exception. Whatever O'Connell's hopes for broad-based support of the repeal agitation, his widely publicised speeches at these great gatherings convinced onlookers that O'Connell was fighting for the Irish nation which, by implication, meant the Catholic nation. Again, economic grievances played their part in this revival of mass politics. Although the *Nation* concentrated on the development of Irish national consciousness, it ran occasional articles demanding land reform, arguing, in particular, that fixity of tenure should be given legal protection. For O'Connell, the solution to all economic problems was the simple one of repeal, and it was only between 1845 and 46 that he outlined a coherent economic programme, which saw him accept the need for a large-scale reform of the land system in Ireland. Still, even then, his economic thinking was governed by the desire to keep state intervention to a minimum, and by his faith in the landowning class.

In 1843, however, he concentrated on the historical grievances under which the Catholic population continued to labour, while cataloguing the failures of the Union. Naturally, such rhetoric sparked concern among Protestants living in Ulster, where it appeared that the Catholic nation was demanding a Catholic state. Indeed, in January 1841, when O'Connell had attempted to raise support for repeal in Belfast, he ran into a storm of opposition. Equally, his strident demands for repeal and the scale of the unparalleled demonstrations in 1843 had forced the Peel administration at Westminster to formulate its response to this new development in Irish nationalism. In 1829 it had bowed to the inevitable and conceded emancipation, but its opposition to repeal was fundamental. In May 1843 Peel told an anxious House of Commons that his government would defend the Union whatever the cost. O'Connell, for his part, appears to have underestimated Peel's determination to stand by the Union, and he continued to raise the stakes in his attempt to break the government's resolve when, in truth, there was no prospect of success. A clash was unavoidable and it came in October 1843. O'Connell's intention was to hold the last of the 1843 series of monster meetings at Clontarf, just outside Dublin. It was planned that this demonstration would be even more impressive than the others, the culmination of a year's campaigning, and preparations to this effect were well under way when the government decided to ban the meeting. Since the beginning of the repeal agitation, Peel had adopted a cautious approach and had rejected calls for coercion. By October 1843, however, he had decided on a definite course of action.

The notices for the Clontarf meeting indicated that it would be more military in character than those that had preceded it, and this gave the government the excuse to issue the proclamation banning it. The Clontarf area was immediately flooded with large numbers of troops to uphold the ban and, fearing bloodshed, O'Connell responded by cancelling the meeting. Such action was in keeping with O'Connell's consistent claims that he would only act constitutionally, but it exposed his earlier words of defiance and threatening language as mere rhetoric. His reputation had taken a blow, but this was partly cushioned by the government's decision to prosecute him for conspiring to cause disaffection. He was jailed in May 1844 but released in September when the House of Lords quashed the sentence on appeal. On his release, the repeal agitation was revived and further demonstrations were organised, but the momentum built up in 1843 was never recovered. Unlike emancipation, the repeal campaign would not end in success, because the government led by Peel, which was in a much stronger position than the Wellington administration in 1829, was determined to do everything in its power to prevent it.

Although he had failed in his bid to deliver repeal, O'Connell had a made a powerful and lasting contribution to Irish nationalism. Clearly influenced by, and in turn influencing, British liberal thinking, he had politicised the masses, demonstrated the power of public opinion, achieved success in electoral politics, and established firm links with one of the two great parties at Westminster. Above all, he had developed a new style of political agitation, which encouraged the masses to participate in these great popular campaigns. While O'Connell courted liberal Protestant support, his leadership undoubtedly strengthened the bonds between constitutional nationalism and the Catholic Church. Unquestionably, this alliance with the church and his rhetoric contributed to the growing polarisation of Irish politics along religious lines. O'Connell was, however, more a product of sectarianism than a cause. Of course, without the involvement of the Catholic Church, neither electoral success nor agitation on such a grand scale would have been possible, though it should be recognised that special circumstances were necessary for the mobilisation of the masses. In return, O'Connell supplied the leadership and discipline which ensured that nationalism would not develop as a challenge to the Catholic Church in Ireland. A high rate of literacy was also a necessary prerequisite for a successful mass movement because, without it, the *Nation* would not have enjoyed such influence. O'Connell understood that the driving forces behind the growth of Irish nationalism in this period were both religious and economic. The Catholic middle classes who were prominent in both the emancipation and repeal campaigns believed that they were suffering under discrimination and, though their position began to improve in the 1830s, this only raised expectations even higher. Although O'Connell enjoyed widespread support during specific periods in the 1830s and 1840s, it was among the more bourgeois elements, both in rural and urban Ireland, that his appeal struck the loudest chord. Similarly, whatever the reality, nationalists believed that the Union had failed to promote economic prosperity, a perception which was compounded by the spectacular economic growth being recorded in contemporary Britain.

While he had not delivered repeal, O'Connell had added substance to the view that the Union was the primary cause of Ireland's problems. Like future nationalist leaders, O'Connell had little understanding of Ulster and he failed to make any real impact in the province. Here, both the religious and economic motors driving constitutional nationalism were largely missing. There were, moreover, other regional variations. Nationalism was strongest in Leinster and Munster, particularly in urban areas where, of course, economic expectations were higher. In spite of the difficulties he faced, O'Connell had introduced the mass of the Irish people to the new idea of democracy and made constitutional nationalism the dominant force in Irish politics, while his influence was felt far beyond Ireland. In the process, he had made Catholics aware of their numerical strength and reminded Protestants of their numerical weakness. O'Connell saw no contradiction between his burning Irish patriotism and his unswerving loyalty to the Crown, and this provided a powerful example for later nationalists in the Home Rule struggle. It was his commitment to constitutionalism that explained his decision to back down in the face of Peel's threat over Clontarf. While O'Connell's action later drew fierce criticism from a small minority of militant nationalists, his decision was based on a clear principle and, though the repeal agitation lost momentum and O'Connell's reputation was damaged, constitutional nationalism survived the setback. Moreover, later generations of Irish nationalists recognised that O'Connell was at his most effective when he combined militant rhetoric with practical politics. It was possible, therefore, for the lines between constitutional and violent nationalism to occasionally become blurred.

In responding to the challenge of O'Connellism, Peel did not confine his policy to cracking down on repeal agitation. He had called O'Connell's bluff at Clontarf, but he intended to follow this display of force with a programme of reform, which might erode O'Connell's support base and reconcile Irish Catholics to the Union. While his reforms were intended to conciliate moderate Catholic opinion, the Prime Minister may also have been keen to promote disunity in the nationalist ranks. In 1844 Peel established a Board of Charitable Bequests, on which Catholics were represented, to facilitate donations to the Catholic Church. In the following year, he increased the annual grant to the Maynooth seminary from £9,000 to £26,000 and made a generous one-off payment of £30,000 for building and repairs. The most significant attempt at conciliation, however, was the 1845 Irish University Act, which proposed the establishment of three Queen's Colleges, in Cork, Galway and Belfast. However, Peel's higher education offer ran into fierce opposition from O'Connell and the Catholic hierarchy, who feared that it would threaten the church's influence on the fundamental issue of education. O'Connell's reaction to the university question immediately created a rift within the repeal movement. The Young Ireland group, particularly Davis, had welcomed Peel's initiative, seeing it as a progressive move which would promote unity among the different denominations or, more particularly, among the educated elite which they represented.

Peel's reforms had the effect of releasing tensions which already existed within Irish nationalism. The Young Ireland group, with a strong Protestant representation among its leadership, favoured a nationalism which was inclusive, in addition to one that had solid cultural foundations. To some extent, it was a clash between idealism and pragmatism. Naturally, this drew the Young Irelanders into conflict with O'Connell. They had clashed over the university question, but Davis's death in September 1845 had created a temporary respite. Nonetheless, O'Connell was unhappy that his authority had been challenged, and he moved to expel the Young Irelanders from the Repeal Association in July 1846, declaring, without any real justification, that they were unwilling to commit themselves to exclusively constitutional methods. Significantly, the Young Irelanders had endorsed the Clontarf decision, but they were critical of O'Connell's more conciliatory stance on his release from prison in September 1844, and their criticism increased with O'Connell's moves to reactivate the Whig alliance towards the end of 1845. With differences in practical politics now added to obvious differences in ideology, a split was inevitable. When it came, both parties were damaged. O'Connell lost the vitality and spirit provided by the Young Ireland intellectuals who, in turn, lost the means of exerting their influence. Only ever a small minority within the Repeal Association, the Young Irelanders faced difficulties in establishing a new organisation able to promote their vision of a more romantic, cultural nationalism. O'Connell's health was now failing, and his powers of judgement were clearly on the wane, but even an O'Connell at the height of his powers would have struggled to maintain the momentum of constitutional nationalism against the background of the famine. By the time of his death in May 1847 constitutional nationalism was largely irrelevant, but O'Connell had established a secure enough foundation to ensure that it would return as a powerful force given the right circumstances.

*Chapter 3*

# The Development of
# Revolutionary Nationalism

ALTHOUGH O'CONNELL CLAIMED TO have exposed the Young Ireland movement's ambivalent attitude towards political violence, it was impossible to envisage these idealistic romantic nationalists engaging in rebellion. Nevertheless, excited by examples of revolution in Europe in 1848 and stung into action by the horrors of the famine, a number of these Young Irelanders stumbled into a confused and futile insurrection. Like the two earlier examples of armed revolution, the 1848 uprising proved a hopeless failure but, taken together, these rebellions established a revolutionary tradition in Irish nationalism and provided an inspiration to later generations of violent nationalists. The 1798 rebellion had been on a much bigger scale and it marked the birth of revolutionary nationalism. The participants in 1798 had sought to establish an independent republic by force of arms, but the insurrection was very badly coordinated and local grievances often acted as a stimulus for rebellion. Two other factors present in 1798 also influenced the course of Irish nationalism. Firstly, the rising had grown out of a form of nationalism which could be described as constitutional separatism, and violence was only contemplated as a last, and hopeless, resort when more conventional political avenues had been closed. This had been a feature in the years immediately preceding 1798, when the radicalising influence of the United Irishmen was suddenly curbed by government repression. Secondly, in spite of heavy northern Presbyterian participation, there were obvious sectarian motives at work in 1798 and, consequently, revolutionary nationalism was equated with Catholic disloyalty in Irish Protestant eyes. This was in spite of the fact that the 1803 rising was actually led by Protestants.

In many ways, the 1803 insurrection led by Robert Emmet was a direct result of the 1798 rebellion. Expelled from Trinity College for his radical views, the young Emmet spent two years in France attempting to secure further military support for a fresh uprising. When this proved unsuccessful, he returned to Ireland and soon engaged with other veterans of 1798 in the planning of a new rising, somehow emerging as the leading conspirator. His plan was to seize Dublin Castle and other important buildings in the capital, a move which, he hoped, would spark a more widespread rebellion in the country at large. What followed, on Saturday 23 July 1803, was a confusing episode, bordering on chaotic farce, as approximately 300 men took to the streets of Dublin. The military planning was thoroughly inadequate and, with such a small force of untrained men at his command, Emmet, who proved a hesitant commander, chose not to attack Dublin Castle, his original target. The small force had occupied two streets when troops arrived and quickly dispersed the insurgents. Emmet fled to County Wicklow, but was captured in the following month and executed on 20 September. The rising, which claimed the lives of about 50 people, had been a catastrophic military failure and it finished the attempts of the remaining United Irish conspirators to plan a further rising. The number of insurgents had been shockingly low and no spontaneous rising had followed in the rest of the country. In spite of its abject failure, however, the 1803 uprising made an important contribution to revolutionary nationalism in Ireland. In his dramatic plea from the dock, Emmet demanded that his epitaph should only be written when Ireland had won her freedom from Britain. This symbolic gesture provided a powerful inspiration for later generations of nationalists, and what might have been remembered as an embarrassing failure was transformed into a heroic act of patriotism which became embedded in the ideology of militant republicanism. In fact, failure itself became a triumph, as the hopelessness of the entire venture, allied to Emmet's youthful, almost innocent idealism, made the 1803 debacle more attractive to future groups of violent nationalists.

Despite its legacy, it would be wrong to place too much importance on events such as the 1803 rebellion. Violent nationalism surfaced only sporadically and, on such occasions, it was characterised by a lack of popular support. Indeed, even the idea of a tradition of revolutionary nationalism appears misleading. Ireland did not have such a tradition of violent nationalism, but it did have a tradition of violence in rural society. Sometimes this was due to vague notions of nationalism, but, more frequently, agrarian unrest was a consequence of local economic grievances. The first half of the nineteenth century witnessed the rapid growth of a host of agrarian secret societies which, as they did during the Tithe War, the name given to the anti-tithe protests of the 1830s, spread chaos in rural Ireland and forced the government to respond with coercive legislation. Nationalism, or even politics, was never the motive for such activities, but clashes with the authorities could easily develop a political dimension. Of these secret societies, the Ribbon organisation was easily the most political in character. It also had an urban base, recruiting among the Dublin artisan class, but its members were drawn from most areas of the country. The Ribbonmen had their origins in the Defender tradition of the late eighteenth century. As such, they were openly sectarian, while adhering to a vague concept of revolutionary nationalism. In Ulster, the Ribbonmen frequently participated in sectarian clashes with their opponents in the Orange Order. Yet, while the sporadic violence perpetrated by all of these secret societies became part of the culture of rural society, the link between their activities and violent nationalism was tenuous. Ribbonism did, nevertheless, advance the concept of an independent Ireland achieved by violent insurrection together with a vague assumption of a social revolution to follow. During specific periods, however, particularly in the late 1820s and early 1840s, O'Connell's militant rhetoric and programme of direct action must have appealed to all shades of militant nationalism, including the various secret societies, thereby demonstrating that there could be considerable overlap between constitutional and revolutionary nationalism. Indeed, during the 1840s, the Young Irelanders made a significant contribution to all three forms of nationalism – constitutional, revolutionary and cultural.

In January 1847 the Young Irelanders who had split with O'Connell formed the Irish Confederation, but it was almost a year before the new body issued a programme outlining its principles. Most importantly, this proclaimed Ireland's right to self-government and reaffirmed a commitment to non-violent methods, thus following closely the original policy of the Repeal Association. However, these lofty political aspirations were irrelevant to an Ireland gripped by famine. The most prominent member of the Irish Confederation was William Smith O'Brien, a liberal in politics from a Protestant gentry background. An MP since 1828, Smith O'Brien had supported emancipation before being persuaded that repeal of the Union was the only solution to Ireland's problems. Of course, Smith

O'Brien was exactly the type of high profile convert, a liberal Protestant with aristocratic connections, that O'Connell was seeking. He was quickly elevated to the top rank of the Repeal Association, which he joined in 1843, serving as leader during O'Connell's term of imprisonment in 1844. Later, Smith O'Brien attempted to heal the divisions between O'Connell and the Young Irelanders but, when the Liberator forced the issue, Smith O'Brien departed with the Young Ireland group to form the Irish Confederation. Influenced by the charismatic Davis, Smith O'Brien wanted to see a reconciliation between Protestants and Catholics in Ireland, which would pave the way for the men of property, such as himself, to play a dominant role in the development of a new form of inclusive nationalism. Only in the last resort, when every other possibility had been exhausted, was Smith O'Brien prepared to contemplate the use of violence for political ends. If the famine sidelined the lofty, idealistic version of Irish nationalism preached by Smith O'Brien, it also encouraged more extreme nationalists on the fringe of the Young Ireland movement who believed that the upheaval in Irish society caused by the agrarian crisis demanded action, and not more political theorising.

Among those who argued that the repeal aim should be abandoned in favour of direct action to save the tenant farming class was James Fintan Lalor. A hitherto obscure figure, who had become associated with the Irish Confederation in 1847, Lalor publicised a programme for agrarian revolution in a number of open letters to the *Nation*. Lalor's proposals involved concerted action by Ireland's tenant farmers, who would refuse to pay rents until the landlords accepted the principle of co-ownership between landlord and tenant. While he was not against the idea of the peasantry imposing their will through force of arms, he argued that his idea of 'moral insurrection' was more suited to contemporary circumstances and claimed that the famine had already done a great deal to undermine the old land system. Though the famine had, in fact, rendered the possibility of such direct action even less likely, Lalor had made a valuable contribution to Irish nationalism by linking it to the struggle between landlord and tenant. His call for a rent strike by small farmers would, he hoped, create the conditions for a successful social and political revolution. Thus, independence would be complemented by the removal of the landlord class and a shift to peasant proprietorship. While he failed to persuade the Irish Confederation to support his initiative, Lalor managed to convince a leading member, John

Mitchel, that by coupling the land issue and the national question, it opened up the prospect of success for revolutionary nationalism. Mitchel, the son of a Unitarian minister from Ulster, was becoming increasingly frustrated by the Confederation's inability to produce a coherent programme of its own to respond to the challenge of the famine. By the end of 1847, he was convinced that only prompt revolutionary action in the form of a peasant-led rebellion could rescue the situation. Withdrawing from the Irish Confederation, Mitchel established a new newspaper, the *United Irishman*, and called for an immediate insurrection to establish an independent Irish republic and address the huge problems facing the country's agrarian underclass. With a number of militant nationalists beginning to side with Mitchel, Smith O'Brien, the senior figure in the Young Ireland movement, tried to hold the line, arguing that only constitutional action should be contemplated and hoping that the landlord class would back his renewed call for the repeal of the Union.

Although Smith O'Brien had openly rejected Mitchel's violent radicalism, the stunning success of French revolutionaries in February 1848 had caused Young Irelanders, who had consistently looked to nationalist movements in Europe for inspiration, to reassess Mitchel's extremist programme. Subsequently, the euphoria created by events on the continent, and the increasing sense of desperation caused by the experience of famine, forced the former moderates within the Young Ireland movement to consider the prospects for an Irish revolution. The government was aware of these developments and Mitchel, Smith O'Brien and Thomas Francis Meagher, another militant who had been the loudest critic of O'Connell's peace resolutions in 1846, were arrested in the spring of 1848. Brought to trial in May, Meagher and Smith O'Brien were released amid scenes of great celebration, but Mitchel was found guilty of treason-felony, a new offence introduced only weeks earlier, and transported. Escaping from Tasmania to America in 1853, Mitchel became involved in Irish-American politics, and his famous *Jail Journal*, which was to have a powerful impact on later nationalist thinking, was published in 1854. In 1875 he returned to Ireland and immediately became involved in politics, winning the Westminster seat of County Tipperary shortly before his death, a victory which was partly attributable to Mitchel's martyr status following his transportation to Australia.

Later, the cautious Smith O'Brien returned to his Limerick estate, but, in July, he decided to tour the country in an attempt to gauge the level of support for revolution. Before this task had been completed, however, the government again moved quickly to arrest prominent figures, including Meagher and Gavan Duffy. This had been made possible by emergency legislation, temporarily suspending habeas corpus, which had been rushed through Parliament in July. Smith O'Brien was still dithering about the prospects for a rebellion when the arrests were made, and he was now faced with the choice of fleeing from arrest or launching an insurrection. While he was extremely nervous about committing his followers to a rebellion, he became convinced, following urgent discussions with Meagher and John Blake Dillon, that their honour would only be saved by taking up arms.

Smith O'Brien was a reluctant and unlikely revolutionary leader. He had only committed himself to revolution when the government had arrested leading Young Ireland militants and banned the Confederate Clubs that had sprung up in the summer of 1847. Together with Meagher and Dillon, Smith O'Brien sought to rally the peasantry in the south of the country, a demoralising venture at a time when the rural poor were obviously more concerned with survival. By 29 July 1848, Smith O'Brien and about 50 followers had congregated near Ballingarry, County Tipperary, and a confrontation ensued between the small band of Young Ireland rebels and members of the Irish Constabulary. In what became known as the 'battle of the Widow McCormack's cabbage patch', armed police, who had taken refuge in Mrs McCormack's house, easily dispersed the insurgents. Smith O'Brien had proved himself an ineffective leader of a hopelessly disorganised rebellion, and he was arrested as he made his way back to County Limerick. Along with other leading figures who had been arrested, Smith O'Brien was convicted of high treason and transported to Tasmania. A number of younger insurgents evaded the authorities and some, notably James Stephens and John O'Mahony, escaped to France where they engaged with fellow revolutionaries and provided a direct link between the Young Ireland rebels and the subsequent Fenian movement. The timing of the insurrection was suicidal, as the famine ensured that the rebellion would not enjoy any degree of popular support. Like 1803, the tiny number of committed revolutionaries was illuminating but, in spite of this, the 1848 rising took its place in the sequence of unsuccessful rebellions and served both as an inspiration and an example to future generations of revolutionary nationalists. Yet its main legacy was not the unmitigated military fiasco but its contribution to the development of a greater sense of nationality among the politically conscious. In the process, these expressions of cultural nationalism were given a sharp political edge.

While the famine guaranteed the failure of the Young Ireland rising, it also had a major impact on the future course of Irish nationalism. In fact, the Young Ireland movement failed to identify with the suffering of the agrarian underclass during the famine, choosing to concentrate on its cultural and political objectives rather than committing itself to any large-scale humanitarian relief effort. In this sense the approach of the Young Irelanders mirrored that of constitutional nationalists in general. In the general election of August 1847 the famine did not feature prominently. Instead, election addresses highlighted repeal and civil and religious liberty as the chief concerns. Of course, the main crisis unfolded soon after this, but the lack of attention paid to the famine during the election campaign is striking.

Still, the scale of the suffering and the Westminster government's inadequate and callous response to the catastrophe were to become ingrained in the Irish national psyche. It did not, however, create anti-English sentiment. This already existed and had, of course, been exploited by O'Connell, but the famine undoubtedly strengthened anti-English feeling and gave it a more precise *raison d'être*. The famine also produced a huge diaspora, and it was among this body that Mitchel's later writings, which charged the British government with genocide, received most attention. Consequently, the quest for vengeance exerted a powerful influence among Irish-Americans, and this was subsequently translated into support for violent nationalism. In Ireland, moreover, both constitutional and revolutionary nationalists regularly used the memory of the famine in their attempts to mobilise support. In this development Lalor's writings continued to reach a wide audience. His views had motivated Young Ireland insurgents and, more than any other writer of the Young Ireland era, Lalor had forged an unbreakable link between the land and the national questions which provided the basis for the advance of nationalist thinking in the Parnellite period. Indeed, it was this merger of economic and political forces which gave nationalism a new vitality in the second half of the nineteenth century.

Yet the famine did not produce an immediate boost for Irish nationalism. It ended mass agitation for repeal and, though the land question had become a central issue in Irish politics, it was to be some time before a new movement with significant popular support emerged. One difficulty was the creation of a nationwide organisation which would enjoy sustainable, long-term support based on the various local concerns and grievances present in the immediate post-famine period. Some attempt to respond to this problem was made in August 1850, when the Irish Tenant League was formed to protect tenant interests. Specifically, the new organisation was established to campaign for the 'three Fs': fair rents, which would be independently fixed; fixity of tenure, which would prevent evictions so long as a tenant paid his rent; and free sale, which would allow a tenant to be compensated for improvements he had made to his holding. This Irish Tenant League had grown out of the great agrarian crisis, as those farmers who had survived the famine were faced with weak agricultural prices and the growing threat of eviction, and the intention was to build up an independent parliamentary party which would fight for tenant protection at Westminster. Further encouragement was offered by the 1850 Irish Franchise Act, which more than doubled the electorate, and, following the general election of 1852, 48 MPs took a pledge to act independently and oppose any government that refused concessions to Ireland on the land question. This Independent Opposition party demonstrated its potential in December 1852, when it helped to topple the minority Conservative government. However, it lacked any real discipline and was quickly torn apart by internal bickering. The rapid demise of the Independent Opposition party in the late 1850s ended the possibility of concerted political action aimed at redressing particular agrarian grievances, but it was the steady recovery in agricultural prices which sharply reduced the level of tenant agitation.

Significantly, this setback for constitutional politics in the late 1850s coincided with the growth of a much more militant form of nationalism. The Fenian movement was also a direct consequence of the 1848 rising. It was founded by some of the 1848 participants who were determined to erase the memory of the Young Ireland rebellion and present a more formidable challenge to British rule in Ireland. The key figures were James Stephens and John O'Mahony, both of whom had fled to Paris following the collapse of the rising. Here they came under the influence of revolutionary societies on the continent and this persuaded them to consider the establishment of a centrally directed, oath-bound secret society, which would be based on the cell structure to safeguard internal security. Stephens had returned to Ireland in 1856 and was soon in contact with radical political elements, particularly in the south-west of the country. At the end of 1853, O'Mahony had left Paris for America where he sought to channel bitterness towards England into support for revolutionary action in Ireland. With encouragement from O'Mahony and guarantees of Irish-American support, Stephens founded the Irish Republican Brotherhood (IRB) in March 1858, though the term Fenians was more commonly used, and immediately began the task of swearing in members.

While the new movement built on the secret society tradition in Ireland, the Fenians articulated a clear political goal in their desire to establish an independent Irish republic. There was also a rejection of constitutionalism and a commitment to the use of violence to achieve this goal, together with an understanding that the Fenian movement had to be ready to seize any opportunity that presented itself. For the movement's leadership, this concept of revolutionary readiness formed a key component in Fenian ideology. While many of its rank and file members probably lacked this revolutionary zeal, the fact that Fenianism should be ready to take advantage of English difficulties, particularly if, as its leaders anticipated, England went to war with France, was central to an understanding of the movement's formation. In theory, the Fenian movement was non-sectarian and anti-clerical, though the fact that most of its membership was Catholic meant that the organisation was never wholly secular. It claimed a direct link with the United Irishmen and subscribed to Davis's vision of an inclusive nationalism, but it never attracted anything like a significant number of Protestants and failed to develop a following among Ulster Presbyterians. The movement also faced fierce opposition from the Catholic Church, which had always been hostile to Catholics joining any secret, oath-bound organisation. Much of this opposition emanated from Paul Cullen, the Archbishop of Dublin, who regarded Fenianism as a direct challenge to the church's authority and viewed revolutionary activity as an attack on religion. Cullen, who became Ireland's first cardinal in 1866, was unequivocal in his opposition to Fenianism, and he received powerful support from a number of senior figures in the Catholic hierarchy, notably from Bishop David Moriarty of Kerry.

Yet, in spite of such powerful clerical opposition, the Fenian movement was beginning to expand. It was strongest in urban centres, where it attracted support among the artisans and petty bourgeoisie. These craftsmen, clerks, teachers and shop assistants were independently-minded people, for whom advancement, either political or social, was problematic. Many of these new recruits were their own masters and they had the time to indulge in an organisation whose secrecy and rituals offered the potential for the occasional exciting evening in what was, otherwise, a fairly dreary existence. Indeed, in many towns the Fenian movement played a prominent role in the organisation of a variety of social and recreational pastimes, and this aspect alone may have been sufficient to attract interested members. Where it made inroads in rural Ireland, the Fenians made most appeal to the poorer tenant farmers and the landless labourers. Taking their cue from Lalor, the Fenians repeated the slogan 'the land for the people', striking a chord in selected areas where Ribbonism had been strong.

Added publicity for the Fenian movement came with the carefully staged funeral of Terence Bellew MacManus, a Young Ireland veteran who died in San Francisco in 1861. American Fenians decided to exhume the body and ship it back to Dublin, where a public row broke out between Archbishop Cullen and the MacManus Committee, the Fenian front organisation with responsibility for coordinating the event in Ireland. Seeing the entire episode as a Fenian publicity stunt, Cullen refused to allow the body to lie in state in Dublin's Pro-Cathedral, and a stand off between the Fenians and the Catholic Church ensued. However, Cullen was defied when Father Lavelle, a priest with strong Fenian sympathies, performed the religious duties at the funeral. In fact, the whole affair caught the public's imagination and a huge crowd lined the funeral route to Glasnevin. The MacManus episode demonstrated that Fenianism could overcome clerical opposition. This was confirmed with the launch of the National Association in 1864. Backed by Cullen and most of the hierarchy, the National Association was a moderate constitutional nationalist body built on O'Connellite principles, but under tight clerical control. Yet it had very little impact on Irish society and failed to halt the spread of Fenianism. By the mid-1860s the Fenian movement had 50,000 members, though Fenian claims frequently exaggerated this figure, and it was undoubtedly successful in rekindling political activity in many areas of the country following the collapse of O'Connellism and the upheaval of the famine. In achieving this success, Fenianism was able to respond to structural changes in post-famine society, and it managed to articulate the feelings and frustrations of the petty bourgeois elements which dominated the movement. Through the *Irish People*, founded in 1863, the movement openly touted for new recruits, while publicising its revolutionary ideas and demanding that the Catholic Church stay out of politics. Of course, the Fenian movement's relationship with the church was complex. By the late 1860s the lower clergy's attitude was frequently ambiguous, and a significant number of priests at parish level were openly sympathetic to the movement.

Not surprisingly, the movement's propaganda impact and its success in attracting new recruits drew it to the attention of the government, which had, hitherto, adopted a low-key attitude to Fenian activities. In September 1865 the government finally acted by suppressing the *Irish People* and arresting Charles Kickham, Thomas Clarke Luby and John O'Leary, the main contributors to the Fenian newspaper. Stephens had escaped arrest, but he hesitated over calling a rebellion. The IRB leadership, and Stephens in particular, had been promising a rebellion, and this was anticipated in 1865, when the organisation appeared ready to engage in revolution. The end of the American Civil War in 1865, in which Irish regiments had played a prominent role, saw the arrival in Ireland of more than 100 soldiers who had fought in the conflict and were now pressing for a rebellion. Still, the arrest of key figures in September had caused confusion, and Stephens himself was in custody by November, though, with the aid of Fenian sympathisers, he escaped within a fortnight. Hiding in a Dublin safe house, Stephens, in spite of pleas from his colleagues, still refused to sanction a rebellion.

At the same time, the government, through its network of informers, was building up a clear picture of the movement's intentions, and its move to suspend habeas corpus in February 1866 was immediately followed by a wave of arrests, which threw Fenianism into disarray. Stephens fled Ireland and arrived in America in May 1866, and here he faced the formidable task of healing a serious internal split in the American branch of the brotherhood. One group wanted to plan an invasion of Canada, but Stephens argued forcefully that American Fenians must support a rising in Ireland, which, he promised, would be launched before the end of 1866. By this stage, however, his American lieutenants were becoming disillusioned with Stephens and his private insistence on the postponement of a rebellion until a more suitable moment. This quickly developed into open warfare and, following a series of meetings in New York in December 1866,

Stephens was removed from the leadership and replaced by Colonel TJ Kelly, a native of Galway and veteran of the Civil War. Almost immediately, Kelly left America with other civil war veterans. His destination was not Ireland but Britain, where Kelly and his associates assumed that they could conduct final preparations for a rising without interference from the authorities. Arriving in London at the end of January 1867, Kelly learned that Fenian elements among the Irish population in Britain had already drawn up their own plan of action. Problems occurred, however, when an arms raid on Chester Castle in February had to be aborted at the last minute on the discovery that the garrison guarding the castle had been reinforced following a tip-off.

Attention then switched to Ireland where, in Stephens's absence, the brotherhood was determined to launch the long-awaited rebellion. In February, a brief skirmish took place in County Kerry, and this was followed on the night of 5th/6th March by a series of minor risings in Dublin, Tipperary, Cork, Limerick, Clare and Wicklow. The failure to coordinate these actions, the damage caused by informers, severe snow storms and resolute action by government forces combined to ensure that the rebellion would end in defeat. Mopping up operations continued over the next few weeks, but the Fenian rising of 1867 had caused very little loss of life, thereby confirming that it was more of a gesture by impatient Fenian activists, whose morale had been sapped by repeated postponements, than a serious attempt to drive the British out of Ireland. But the collapse of the rising did not mean the end of the Fenian organisation, which retained considerable support in Ireland, America and Britain. Kelly was still active in England, but he was arrested in Manchester in September after being spotted acting suspiciously in a doorway. One week later, as he was being transported between the jail and the local court, an armed Fenian gang trying to rescue Kelly attacked his carriage. In the ensuing melee an unarmed policeman was shot dead and, following a number of subsequent arrests, three Fenian volunteers were tried for their role in the raid and executed on 24 November 1867. The execution of these 'Manchester Martyrs' stirred passions right across nationalist Ireland. The embarrassing failure of the attempted rebellion was quickly forgotten, as an outpouring of sympathy helped to ensure the survival of Fenianism. The Catholic Church, previously hostile to the organisation, condemned the executions and organised commemorative masses, which were held in different parts of Ireland. Fenianism had provided violent nationalism with a new group of martyrs, while adding to the sequence of failed insurrections.

Yet more than previous examples of revolutionary nationalism, Fenianism was strongly identified with the use of physical force. Although the stipulated goal was an Irish republic, it was true that many Fenian activists did not dwell on the precise nature of such a constitutional change, but were really separatist nationalists who simply wanted as much freedom as possible for Ireland. While their movement had been infiltrated by government agents, Fenians themselves were keen to infiltrate other nationalist organisations and influence their direction. Their contribution to the development of a more militant form of nationalism was also enhanced by their association with their American sister organisation, which stood ready to provide the necessary support to make armed insurrection in Ireland a reality. At the heart of the Fenian movement, however, was its commitment to an insurrection planned by revolutionary conspirators. This legacy of revolutionary conspiracy was, of course, most famously revealed in 1916. The activities of the Fenian movement also forced the government to move the Irish question up its list of priorities. This was guaranteed when, in December 1867, a plan was devised to spring an important Fenian activist, Richard Burke, from Clerkenwell prison in London. In an attempt to blast a hole in the prison wall, the Fenian gang killed twenty innocent Londoners. Public opinion in England was outraged, as the atrocity forced the Westminster government of the day to give serious attention to Ireland.

But the impact of Fenianism was also felt outside the narrow confines of revolutionary nationalism. In making contact with like-minded nationalists on his return to Ireland in 1856, Stephens had met members of the Phoenix literary societies. These nationalist clubs, the most famous of which was the Phoenix Society founded in Skibbereen, County Cork, by Jeremiah O'Donovan Rossa, focused on the revival of Gaelic culture, but lively political discussion generated by advanced nationalist thinking was a fundamental part of life in these emerging literary and political groups. The new Fenian organisation soon absorbed the Phoenix Society and this, together with the contribution made by O'Donovan Rossa, Charles Kickham and other 'literary Fenians', gave the movement a cultural dimension, which appealed, in particular, to the petty bourgeoisie. Fenianism, moreover, provided the vehicle for many members of this lower middle class to develop a growing sense of self-respect. In particular, it appealed to independent-minded individuals who refused to recognise their social betters, or to accept the prevailing deference so common in contemporary Irish society. In this way, the Fenian movement was much more than a revolutionary organisation with a clearly defined political goal. It attracted men who aspired to the creation of a more egalitarian society in which self-reliance was a pronounced feature. From its formation there was also a subliminal political task for the organisation. Many activists believed that the Fenian movement had to complete the process of politicisation by preparing the nation for freedom. This was, of course, an extension of the work begun by Young Ireland.

Fenianism also built on the tradition of the agrarian secret society in Ireland and, almost inevitably, the movement was drawn to the land question. While it never produced a coherent social programme, it did subscribe to Lalor's anti-landlord thinking and, in time, this helped to push constitutional and revolutionary nationalism closer together. This process was also made possible by the Fenian movement's growing respectability, something that was partly attributable to the easing of clerical hostility to the organisation. Hard evidence of this came in November 1869, when O'Donovan Rossa won the Tipperary by-election while serving a prison sentence for Fenian activities. The by-election victory demonstrated that constitutional and revolutionary nationalism could work together for a common purpose given the right circumstances, and this laid the foundation for nationalist success in the last quarter of the nineteenth century. Ultimately, of course, the overlap of revolutionary and cultural nationalism made a powerful contribution to the Easter Rising in 1916.

*Chapter 4*
# Land and Nationalism

N O UNDERSTANDING OF THE advances made by Irish nationalism in the last quarter of the nineteenth century can take place without an appreciation of the importance of the land question. In these years an alliance was forged between nationalists and tenant farmers that lasted well into the twentieth century. The demand for lower rents, and ultimately peasant proprietorship, became absorbed into the wider campaign for self-government. Landlord-tenant relations acquired a new political dimension, as Irish nationalism became much more closely identified with a specific economic grievance. The emergence of the land question in a new format was linked to changes in agriculture, many of which were the result of the famine. Whereas the social structure of rural Ireland before the famine comprised landlords, farmers and labourers, this had largely been reduced to just landlords and tenants in the second half of the century. The famine had decimated those on the bottom rung of the social ladder, and the number of landless labourers in rural Ireland declined further from 700,000 in 1851 to 260,000 by the end of the century. This paved the way for a more direct confrontation between landlord and tenant. The tenant farming class was much stronger in the post-famine period. The 1861 census revealed that 40 per cent of the land was held in farms of 100 acres or more, and tenant farmers enjoyed a significant increase in earnings in the third quarter of the century. Livestock prices rose sharply in this period, and a combination of prices and wages paid to tenant farmers rose by 62 per cent between the 1850s and 1870s. During the same period, moreover, rents only increased by an average of 20 per cent, meaning that in real terms tenant farmers were much better off.

At the same time, however, the landlord class had also staged a recovery after the famine. While a number of impoverished landlords took advantage of the 1849 Encumbered Estates Act to sell their property, there were still approximately 10,000 landlords in Ireland in 1851. This gentry class also benefited from the post-famine economic boom and the continuation of deferential politics. Indeed, the electoral success of the Irish Tory party during these decades provided further evidence of the upturn in the landed class's political fortunes following the challenges of the O'Connell era. The absence of any major nationalist agitation after the famine was another significant factor accounting for the continued social and political hegemony of the landlords. Although the number of landlords who were MPs fell from 73 in 1868 to 52 in 1874, they still retained great power, particularly at local level where they dominated the Grand Juries and poor law boards. Of course, the public image of these landlords was of a privileged elite who rarely displayed any sympathy for their tenants. Yet recent historical research has rejected the simple notion of a rackrenting gentry class eager to evict any tenant who fell behind with his rent. In theory, most tenants could have their rents increased on an annual basis, and they generally had no claims for compensation on any improvements that they carried out on their holdings until the 1870 Land Act. In practice, however, rent increases were modest, while evictions rarely exceeded one for every 1,000 holdings in most years. Still, the impact of evictions had a powerful effect on the Irish psyche. Some 90,000 evictions were recorded by the RIC between 1847 and 1880, though more than half of these took place from 1847–50. Naturally, the circumstances surrounding many of the evictions in the famine period had blighted the reputation of the landlords. Furthermore, evictions were very public affairs, often involving the forces of the Crown, and this added to the image of a downtrodden peasantry labouring under a rapacious landed elite that could call upon the full power of the British state to assert its authority. Of course, perception was, in this instance, more important than reality. When this was supplemented by the memory of the misery and despair associated with evictions during the famine, it becomes easy to see why the fear of eviction was such a powerful emotion among the tenant farming class.

It was true, however that the famine had presented the landlords with the opportunity to remove the smallholders on their estates. This trend towards consolidation had begun before the famine, but the catastrophic failure of the potato crop enabled the landlords to accelerate the consolidation of farms into more profitable holdings in which livestock farming would replace subsistence agriculture. Another feature of rural society that was misconstrued in post-famine Ireland was the level of agrarian crime. Like evictions, agrarian crime attracted a great deal of publicity, but it really only comprised a small fraction of total crime. It was also true that less than 50 per cent of the 'outrages' were directly linked to disputes between landlords and tenants. More common were family rows and disputes between neighbouring tenant farmers, which often resulted in intimidation and violence. While no part of the country was immune to instances of agrarian crime, it was apparent that it was less significant in Ulster. In fact, due to a combination of the impact of the Ulster custom, the importance of the flax crop, the proximity of Belfast, which had become a very good market for produce, and the better soil, Ulster counties were relatively free from agrarian crime. Other areas of the country, however, did not enjoy these advantages, and this increased the likelihood of tension between landlord and tenant. On occasion, this could result in a spectacular outrage, such as the murder of the Earl of Leitrim in 1878, which contributed to the impression of a rural society simmering on the verge of violent upheaval. This was a misinterpretation shared by many of the leading political figures at Westminster. Here, the Irish landlord was consistently held to be a major cause of most Irish problems. Yet, while the Irish gentry did not invest as much capital in their property as their English counterparts, many were actually good landlords who co-operated fully with their tenants for mutual benefit. By the late 1870s, however, circumstances combined in a manner that cast the landed class as the enemy of the people. A new wave of agrarian agitation followed, but what transformed the situation was that powerful political undercurrents were now operating.

This focus on the land question highlighted the economic grievance that provided the momentum for Irish nationalism in the last quarter of the nineteenth century. The landlord class was stereotyped as alien, differing in religion and nationality from the vast bulk of the tenant farmers, even though Catholic landlords owned almost 15 per cent of Irish land. This enabled the various strata in rural Ireland, ranging from the well off grazier to the landless labourer, to unite against the discredited landlords in the expectation that their action would lead to radical social change based on an overhaul of the land system. By channelling this agrarian discontent into support for a new and more dynamic form of nationalism, the tenant farmers, the largest group in Irish society, were mobilised to fight for economic and political change. In O'Connell's era, economic grievances had been a factor in the mobilisation of the peasantry and, in the 1850s, the 'tenant right' movement had attracted a measure of support by campaigning for the three Fs, but no real progress on the land question had been made. This would change towards the end of the century as a revitalised nationalist movement, resuscitated by land agitation, pressed the case for reform at Westminster. There, too, there was some ground for optimism. William Ewart Gladstone, the new Liberal Prime Minister, had, mainly because of the Fenian rising, taken a keen interest in Ireland and was determined to introduce measures, which he hoped would improve the situation sufficiently to erode support for violent nationalism. In 1869 his Irish Church Act, which disestablished the Church of Ireland, acknowledged Catholic numbers, though it was bitterly opposed by Irish Protestants. His 1870 Land Act, which gave legal recognition to the 'Ulster custom' by compensating an outgoing tenant for improvements, made little impact, but it was given subsequent symbolic endorsement as it became the first in a celebrated series of land reforms. Prior to this the sale of a tenant's interest in a holding was possible on certain estates outside Ulster, but the whole question of 'tenant right' was very complex.

The formation of the Amnesty Association in June 1869 was of more significance for the development of nationalism. Organised to campaign for the release of Fenian prisoners, the association chose the well-known barrister, Isaac Butt, as its president. Butt had defended many of the Fenian leaders during a series of high profile trials after the rising, and he went on to address a number of public meetings on behalf of the association. While Butt was the figurehead, the real driving force in the movement was its secretary, John Nolan. He organised the great public gatherings in the late summer of 1869, which rekindled memories of O'Connell's monster meetings earlier in the century. In October a crowd estimated at 200,000 turned out for a rally at Cabra near Dublin, but these demonstrations were subsequently suspended, as the movement's leaders feared the development of another Clontarf. Some success was achieved with the release of a number of minor figures, but the real significance of the Amnesty Association was the collaboration between constitutional nationalists like Butt and the Fenians who were active in the movement. Indeed, the Amnesty Association quickly developed as something of an umbrella organisation, attracting both moderates and rank and file Fenians, and it was clearly successful in mobilising significant support for a political cause.

While Butt had understood the motivation of revolutionary nationalists, he was an unequivocal opponent of political violence and sought, therefore, to divert the Fenian movement down a more constitutional route. Stephens had always opposed such a dilution of revolutionary principles, but his removal, and subsequent repudiation, had opened up the prospect of a more flexible approach by the new Fenian leadership. The result was Fenian approval for Butt's Home Government Association, formed in 1870 to promote the demand for a new parliament in Dublin. Evidence that the Fenian movement was becoming less constrained by its purist principles appeared in January of that year, when the Supreme Council of the IRB directed its members to seek local government office. In 1873 the Home Government Association, really no more than a comfortable, middle class talking shop, was dissolved and a new organisation, the Home Rule League, took its place. By this stage the need for more effective organisation had been recognised, and the demand for Home Rule had aroused interest among a growing number of the Catholic clergy. Moreover, the Fenian movement had added its tentative support to Butt's new venture. Following a decision of the Supreme Council, Butt was informed that the Fenians would play a supporting role for a period of three years in an attempt to win a Home Rule parliament for Ireland. This was a bonus, because it was clear to Butt that the Fenian organisation had the capacity to arouse national consciousness, and he was eager to take advantage of this in promoting his new movement. Progress in this direction would also give Butt the chance to shepherd Fenianism away from violence and the emerging Home Rule movement attracted Fenian activists. While it was never a separatist body, rank and file Fenians, who were weary of the rigid constraints demanded by their oath, accepted that Home Rule was, at least, a move in the right direction. Fenians certainly were prominent at elections, notably in Butt's own by-election victory in September 1871, as they provided the drive and enthusiasm at local level to marshal electoral support. Still, the experience of the Amnesty Association had shown that leading republicans such as Nolan were impatient with Butt's cautious approach, indicating that their long-term commitment would depend on the Home Rule movement adopting a more radical stance.

Almost immediately, the Home Rule League was presented with an opportunity to test its support, when a general election was called at the beginning of 1874. Butt's efforts were rewarded with the return of 59 Home Rule MPs, though this figure was misleading. At the previous general election the Liberals had been the dominant party in Ireland, winning two-thirds of the country's 105 seats, and a significant number of new Home Rulers, as they became known, were former Liberals who only adopted the Home Rule tag to ensure their return to Parliament. In reality, there were only about 20 who were genuinely committed to the Home Rule cause. Still, Butt had made an impressive beginning, but he was unable to turn this initial electoral success in Ireland to any real advantage at Westminster. When he did attend Parliament, Butt was keen to engage in logical and reasoned argument in an attempt to persuade the House of Commons that a devolved scheme of government would bring benefits to both Britain and Ireland. His case, though eloquently delivered, was swiftly rejected by the new Conservative government led by Benjamin Disraeli, and the genteel Butt was content to accept the status quo. In addition, Butt failed to provide the type of strong leadership necessary to hold together the disparate Home Rule group at Westminster, and it soon split into a number of disorganised factions. Undoubtedly, his politeness and ineffectiveness undermined Butt's reputation with those Fenians who had been prepared to give constitutionalism a chance. These men were more impressed by the activities of a small group of more militant Home Rulers who refused to be constrained by Butt's moderation. The key activist among these militants was Joseph Biggar, a prosperous Belfast provision merchant, who had been elected MP for Cavan in 1874.

Biggar paid no respect to the niceties of parliamentary politics. From 1875 to 1877 Biggar orchestrated a campaign of 'parliamentary obstruction' in which he and his associates exploited every opportunity to delay business in the House of Commons. Though only a handful of Home Rulers were involved, they could, by carefully coordinating their activities, bring the House to a standstill. Of course, their actions infuriated other MPs and made them extremely unpopular at Westminster, but they did fire popular interest in Ireland. In 1875 Biggar actually joined the Fenian movement and, in the following year, he was elevated to the organisation's ruling body, the IRB Supreme Council, where he joined another MP, John O'Connor Power, who had become MP for Mayo in 1874. Although their refusal to leave Parliament led to the expulsion of both Biggar and O'Connor

Power from the Fenian movement in 1877, when the Supreme Council, by a majority of just one vote, suspended its cooperation with the Home Rulers, the actions of these constitutional Fenians had given the Home Rule movement a cutting edge. The most important figures engaged with Biggar in impeding parliamentary business were O'Connor Power and the MP for Limerick, WH O'Sullivan.

It was the strategy of parliamentary obstruction which first brought Charles Stewart Parnell to prominence. Parnell was an Anglo-Irish Protestant landlord from County Wicklow, who had been returned as an MP for County Meath at a by-election in April 1875. While his family had been active in public life for 100 years, Parnell himself had little political experience and, initially at least, there was little to suggest that he would become the dominant figure in the Home Rule party. From his American mother he had inherited a deep-seated antipathy to England, and his experiences as an undergraduate at Cambridge reinforced this prejudice. Although he was not a gifted public speaker in the Butt mould, Parnell's social standing gave him a natural self-confidence, and he was dismissive of the formalities at Westminster and never in awe of fellow MPs, many of whom, of course, shared his social background. Ruffling parliamentary feathers did not worry Parnell, and his participation in the obstruction campaign raised his profile in Ireland. For Parnell, obstruction was a simple device for creating interest and maintaining morale in Ireland, and the frequent denunciation of Parnell, Biggar and the others achieved his objective. Of course, an embarrassed Butt joined in the criticism of Parnell and the tactic of obstruction. Having had his argument for Home Rule rejected at Westminster, Butt was content to wait on the sidelines expecting sympathy from British MPs who could eventually be persuaded of the logic behind a Home Rule solution. Parnell was frustrated by this lack of activity and by Butt's apparent lack of enthusiasm for political struggle, and he soon became a rival for the leadership.

By the late 1870s nationalism was about to enter a new phase in which a more dynamic, grass roots movement would emerge to demand a mixture of far-reaching economic and political reforms. The decade after the famine had witnessed the emergence of an agrarian-political alliance, but it was short-lived and failed to make a real impact. The Irish Tenant League was established in Dublin in August 1850, and it promoted the demand for the three Fs. From the outset the movement drew clerical support, as

Presbyterian ministers in the north joined the Catholic lower clergy in the south in leading the demand for land reform at local level. At the same time, the extension of the franchise in 1850, which increased the Irish electorate from 45,000 to 164,000, had sufficient impact to persuade the Tenant League to back the creation of an Independent Opposition party. The new party won more than 40 seats at the 1852 general election, but it was unable to attract support for the cause of agrarian reform at Westminster. By the end of the decade the Irish Tenant League had been wound up, and the Independent party, though retaining some appeal at the polls, was subsequently torn apart by a series of internal splits. Perhaps the principal reason for the difficulties in developing this agrarian-political alliance, however, was the economic upturn in the mid-1850s, which naturally took the edge off agrarian agitation.

The increased prosperity was, of course, linked to the consolidation of holdings, and this meant that the stronger farmers tended to increase both in number and in importance. Further changes occurred with the shift from arable to pastoral farming, a development pushed by the stronger farmers who had some access to capital. Profit was the motivation for this switch to pasture, as the increasing volatility in the price of cereals and the sharp rise in foreign competition made livestock farming more attractive. Yet there were marked regional differences in the overall pattern of development. The move away from tillage and the consolidation of holdings combined to create large grazing 'ranches' in the east and midlands, but these changes made less impact in the west. Although subsistence farming had given way to commercial farming over most of the country, Connacht still had large numbers of cottiers and small farmers who continued to rely on the potato. Yet, even in the west, these smallholdings were interspersed with a number of large ranches, thus creating the conditions for tension between the grazier and small farmer. When this was added to the existing strained relationship between landlord and tenant, rural society in the west was characterised by a complex mix of social tension. Pressure on the land continued to be a feature of rural society in Connacht. While it suffered more during the famine than any other province, Connacht emigration rates only caught up with the national average in 1870, and the rate of population decrease was also much lower in Connacht in the 30 years after the famine, as the move away from the pattern of early marriages was delayed in the west.

It was no surprise, therefore, that the agricultural depression, which began in 1877 and affected the whole country, was most keenly felt in Connacht. A combination of a poor potato crop and a worldwide depression, conditions which prevailed in the following two years, produced the most serious and sustained agricultural depression since the famine. A prolonged period of poor weather exacerbated the deteriorating situation and, by 1879, the prospect of another famine became a reality for many of the west's poorest farmers. At the same time, the slump in cattle prices hit both the smallholder who reared cattle and the grazier who purchased these animals for finishing. Nowhere were these factors more important than in County Mayo, which had a strong tradition of tenant organisation. Livestock farming had become increasingly important in a county where the move to cattle was already under way before the famine. Even poor farmers, whose staple diet remained the potato, could derive some benefit from the cattle boom by rearing a few livestock on marginal land and then selling them to the large graziers. Many of the county's graziers were actually shopkeepers, publicans, merchants and professional men from the towns, who rented the best local agricultural land and employed stockmen to look after their livestock interests. Previously, relations between this rural bourgeoisie and the poorer farmers had been difficult, but the agricultural crisis of 1877–79 united these different social groups for a brief period. Indeed, the land agitation had a rhetoric of liberty, and the socially inclusive language of nationalism could foster the interests of the strong farmers who were so prominent in the agitation, while simultaneously mobilising the landless labourers to claim their own rights. Spurred on by the threat of mass evictions, the Mayo farming classes came together to challenge the authority of the landlords and demand a reduction in rent. This new wave of economic distress coincided with a rise in agrarian unrest, as an increasingly desperate rural population vented its frustration in the traditional manner. Indeed, the recession was intensified by the sudden drop in demand for seasonal labour in Britain, which had previously offered an outlet for many of the county's poorest families.

The agricultural depression of the late 1870s provided the backdrop to a revival of nationalism, which, while drawing on past experience, was new in form because of its direct association with a particular economic grievance. This had the effect of mobilising the tenant farming classes in the struggle against the alien landlords and a foreign government. Mayo provided the starting point, because a large section of the county's tenant farmers had recently been politicised by an energetic group of leaders who were able to coordinate and direct the agrarian agitation. The election team which had run O'Connor Power's campaign in 1874 had been hard at work in spreading radical ideas which pulled together agrarian and political thinking. O'Connor Power embarked on annual lecture tours which raised political consciousness among his new tenant farmer supporters, and his views were widely endorsed in the local press. The local Fenian movement was also active in the O'Connor Power circle, using its influence to radicalise political thinking in the county. It was this energetic and dynamic local leadership that was able to coordinate the agrarian agitation and give it a political dimension. Previously, the impact of the Amnesty Association and dissatisfaction both with the 1870 Land Act and the failure of Gladstone's government to understand the Irish problem had aroused fresh interest in the political process. O'Connor Power and his colleagues were able to build on this development, and they recognised that land was fast becoming the key political issue in Ireland.

This was the situation that Michael Davitt found when he toured the county in 1878. Davitt was the son of a Mayo tenant farmer who had been evicted from his holding in 1851. Raised in Lancashire where he lost his right arm in a factory accident in 1857, Davitt joined the Fenian movement in England and was jailed in 1870 for his part in a gun-running plot. On his release from Dartmoor prison in December 1877, he rejoined the Fenian movement and was quickly elected to the Supreme Council. Like a number of other leading Fenians, Davitt saw the potential of closer cooperation with the constitutional movement, and in a series of speeches in Ireland and the north of England in the spring of 1878 he advocated a new understanding between separatists and those whom he described as 'honest home rulers'. When he returned to his native Mayo and toured the county, Davitt focused on the ideals of advanced nationalism, as he outlined the separatist goal. But what struck Davitt on his return was the discovery that the Mayo tenant farmers were so far advanced in their approach to the land issue. Soon, he added his energy and organisational ability to the agrarian movement in Mayo. Indeed, Davitt played some part, though not the key role, in the arrangements for the famous Irishtown meeting in April 1879, which attracted a crowd of about 10,000 eager to adopt resolutions demanding a reduction in rents and the abolition of landlordism. While Davitt subsequently claimed the credit, it was, in fact, Clan na Gael, the republican organisation in the United States, that played the key role in promoting the new strategy of cooperation between Fenians and Home Rulers to campaign for self-government supported by aggressive agitation on the land issue.

Parnell did not foresee the agrarian crisis that was to transform the fortunes of the Home Rule party. Indeed, he was slow to respond to the political potential of the agrarian movement in Mayo, rejecting a number of calls to organise an alliance of MPs and land reformers. Although the success of the Irishtown meeting warned Parnell that the tenant agitation in Mayo had the capacity to develop a momentum of its own, he still hesitated. In the end, it was Davitt's persistent prompting that persuaded him to identify with the land issue, and he agreed to attend a second meeting, planned for Westport on 8 June 1879. At the Westport rally Parnell outlined his own views on the land question to another large audience. During the agrarian crisis Parnell had moved tentatively towards Lalor's notion of 'the land for the people', but he was careful to stress that this was a long-term goal. Parnell was firmly opposed to social revolution, and he argued for conciliation with the landlords in his demand for a fair rent, which he defined as one that "the tenant can reasonably pay according to the times". Yet Parnell also appealed to the agrarian radicals by declaring that tenants should "keep a firm grip" on their holdings, if they were threatened with eviction. Still, Parnell's call for direct action was deliberately vague, as he neglected to outline the precise steps that tenant farmers should take to defend their position.

To some extent, therefore, Parnell was feeling his way on the land question. Although he had hesitated before committing himself, Parnell sensed that the growing agrarian unrest in the west had developed into a major political grievance, which he had to bring under control and direct. Furthermore, the agitation in Mayo had enhanced O'Connor Power's leadership claims over the militant wing of the Home Rule party, and Parnell realised that he had to move decisively in order to outmanoeuvre his rival. One thing Parnell understood perfectly was power. While his quarrel with Butt had made him very unpopular with many of his more cautious parliamentary colleagues, his ambition remained undiminished and he was ruthless in his pursuit of power. Butt had died in May 1879, and the Wicklow landlord was determined to replace him and provide the Home Rule party with much more vigorous and dynamic leadership.

In fact, Parnell's path to the leadership was cleared by O'Connor Power's petulance and lack of judgement. On learning that Parnell had been invited to address the Westport meeting, O'Connor Power refused to attend and, in so doing, allowed his rival to reap the political benefit of all the groundwork that he had done on the agrarian issue.

✗ Parnell, to his credit, recognised that the land issue was the key to the national question, and that if he could successfully link the Home Rule movement to a popular demand like land reform, then it could catch fire. It was precisely this belief – that a fundamental link existed between the land and national questions – which lay behind the agreement on the 'New Departure'. The driving force behind the New Departure was John Devoy, the leading figure in the American Fenian movement. Devoy had been jailed for Fenian activities in 1866 and released in 1871 on condition of exile. Soon after his arrival in America Devoy joined Clan na Gael, which had been formed in 1867 in an attempt to heal the divisions in the American Fenian movement. Through his resourcefulness and determination Devoy quickly rose to the leadership of Clan na Gael, and, by the late 1870s, the Clan was the dominant force within Fenianism. In 1876, Devoy's was a key voice in persuading the IRB Supreme Council to end the Fenian dalliance with constitutional nationalism, but the early impression created by Parnell caused him to reconsider this purist Fenian approach. Parnell's participation in the obstruction strategy and his general air of defiance had brought him to Devoy's attention, and Clan na Gael made contact with him in 1877. In the following year Devoy tried to secure Parnell's backing for a new departure style project but, at that point, the Meath MP was not ready to adopt such a risky strategy. By June 1879, however, the rapid emergence of the land issue in Mayo had altered the balance in favour of participation. Joining Devoy for the crucial meeting on 1 June 1879 were Parnell and Davitt, who listened to Devoy's proposals outlining the new strategy. It was based on the understanding that the Home Rule movement would not interfere with possible Fenian rebellion plans and, in return, Clan na Gael would provide political and financial support for Parnell, as he led the campaign for Irish self-government and sought to turn the Home Rule party into a more disciplined political machine. A key figure working behind the scenes to bring about this development was the London-based journalist, JJ O'Kelly, a leading IRB man who became the MP for Roscommon in 1880. A committed Fenian, O'Kelly believed that Ireland would need to undergo a rapid political transformation to create a new 'nationalist public opinion', led by more advanced Nationalist MPs at Westminster. This, he argued, would put Ireland in a better position to take full advantage of a successful Fenian revolution. Crucially, O'Kelly exerted a powerful influence on Devoy. In the autumn of 1878, Devoy acted by authorising arms imports to Ireland, funded by Clan na Gael, and by publishing a political programme in the Irish press without prior consultation with the IRB. Devoy's new proposals were quickly dubbed the 'new departure' programme, and they advocated self-government backed by vigorous land agitation, which they hoped would culminate in peasant proprietorship. It was also clear that both Devoy and O'Kelly were relying on Parnell, the great emerging talent in the Home Rule movement, to provide a much more uncompromising style of leadership.

Underpinning the New Departure was a commitment to vigorous agitation on the land issue, with peasant proprietorship as the stated objective. To some extent O'Connor Power and his associates in Mayo had already prepared the ground for this change in direction, and Devoy was simply recognising the reality of the situation. The New Departure symbolised the alliance between the Home Rule movement, radical agrarianism and Fenianism, and it produced a new mass movement in Irish politics, advancing the cause of nationalism under Parnell's expert leadership. While the compact was very much Devoy's agenda, it was Parnell who gained most from the New Departure. Frustrated by the inactivity of the IRB Supreme Council, whose members were reluctant to allow their separatist philosophy to be contaminated with agrarian issues, Devoy was convinced that Fenians had to participate in the agrarian movement if they were to prevent the land question extinguishing the Fenian flame altogether. At the same time, the Clan na Gael leader believed that the Westminster government would fail to solve the land question, and this would allow the Fenian movement to harness the mass support of mobilised tenant farmers in a new drive for an independent Ireland.

Although he gave the impression that he was in agreement with Devoy's analysis, Parnell's mind was working in a different direction. He sensed that the British government would move on the land question, if sufficient pressure was applied, and this success would fuel support for the political objective of Home Rule. These different interpretations added to the confusion on the outcome of the New Departure. Devoy was convinced that he had Parnell's backing for his separatist programme when, in reality, Parnell had only offered vague assurances of support for Devoy's aim of full independence. In truth, it was more likely that Parnell's participation in the New Departure was motivated by a desire to thwart Devoy's ambition, as he sought, in the short-term, to involve all shades of nationalism in the agrarian struggle and then, in the longer-term, to transfer this energy to the political struggle for Home Rule. While it was true that he had been influenced by Davis and his desire for a more inclusive nationalism, Parnell was no romantic nationalist. Rather, he was a ruthlessly pragmatic politician. Clearly Parnell wanted the support of militant nationalists but he was, at best, ambiguous in any commitments he may have made and gave little in return. Dabbling with Fenian and agrarian radicals may have appeared a risky strategy for Parnell to follow, but it was only by his participation in the New Departure that he was able to restrain militants such as Davitt. Where Devoy and Davitt thought that Parnell was joining them in launching a national revolution, he was steadily tightening his grip on the emerging movement and reining in the more militant elements.

In the summer of 1879, therefore, Parnell's immediate concern was to prevent agrarian agitation spinning out of control. Davitt had launched the Land League of Mayo in August 1879 at a meeting in Castlebar, which Parnell did not attend. The new Mayo organisation, which had very solid roots, boasted a radical programme based on the rallying cry of "the land for the people". By October, Davitt had made the necessary arrangements to develop a national movement, and it was really only at this point that the still cautious Parnell committed himself fully to the land agitation by accepting Davitt's invitation to become President of the Irish National Land League. Significantly, Parnell had used his influence to tone down the new movement's programme. While it continued to adhere to the idea of peasant proprietorship, the real focus was on the short-term objectives of halting evictions and reducing rents.

In fact, the rhetoric of "the land for the people" concealed the sharp divisions that existed between the landless labourers and the stronger tenant farmers. Spreading quickly from its Mayo stronghold, the Land League established a network of branches all over the country and coordinated the campaign against landlordism, though it enjoyed less support in the predominantly Protestant counties in Ulster. In challenging the landlords, the League mobilised the entire agricultural community and drew it inexorably towards nationalism. The League was a truly popular movement, driven from the bottom up, and outside clerical control. It also operated, very clearly, outside parliament. Local grievances were articulated and national solutions offered. The legitimacy of landlordism was questioned, and the dependence of the foreign landlord on a foreign government was repeatedly highlighted. The tactics employed by the League were brilliant and varied. It borrowed heavily from the secret society tradition and, though Parnell frequently urged his followers to use exclusively peaceful methods, violence became an effective tool. At local level the League was frequently led by Fenian activists, though it tended to be members of secret societies, rather than IRB personnel, who were responsible for the violence. Indeed, the launch of the League in October 1879 was followed by an upsurge in the number of agrarian outrages, and the level of violence was sufficient for the period 1879–82 to become known as the 'Land War'. There had, of course, been instances of agrarian crime in the months before the establishment of the League, but the figure escalated sharply in 1880, as shootings, arson and cattle-maiming became commonplace.

It was the combination of poor weather and the collapse of agricultural prices that had precipitated this crisis. Now agrarian outrages rose to unprecedented levels, and approximately 2,500 of these outrages were reported to the RIC during the course of 1880. Evictions also rose sharply, reaching levels not seen since the immediate post-famine period. From 1878–81 landlords issued more than 14,000 eviction decrees in the five counties of Mayo, Galway, Clare, Kerry and Cork. While large areas of the country experienced agrarian violence to some degree, it was more prevalent in these western counties, where anxious smallholders still experienced economic hardship into the 1880s. This agrarian crisis naturally gave further impetus to the Land League, and it attracted 200,000 members in the first two years of its existence. For the tenant farming class the sharp decline in prices was more damaging, because it took place against a backdrop of rising expectations. Tenant farmers had enjoyed greater economic prosperity in the period after the famine, as the pace of wages and prices comfortably outstripped rent increases. The impact of this sudden check on economic expectations was even more striking, because memories of wholesale evictions, and of the famine itself, were so ingrained in the minds of these western farmers. Yet what really transformed the situation in this particular crisis was the leadership supplied by Parnell and

Davitt. This powerful political leadership, supported by Fenian activists at local level, was able to exploit the new wave of agrarian discontent and give it a political voice, which projected it onto the national stage. This was markedly different to the earlier periods of economic distress, such as the early 1860s, when effective leadership failed to emerge, allowing bursts of agrarian agitation to fizzle out as divisions among the various farming strata led to bitter recrimination among the local leaders.

During the period of the Land League, leadership at local level often fell to a prosperous grazier, or a shopkeeper, publican or merchant from a local town, the economic prosperity of which was totally dependent on its immediate agricultural hinterland. In this way a remarkable unity emerged between town and country, as well as between the different social strata in Irish society. Fighting under "the land for the people" banner, the general aim was to transfer ownership of the land from the small group of existing landlords to a much larger number of Irish tenant farmers. Both the method and the precise outcome of such a redistribution were never clearly defined, and this allowed, in the short-term at least, the establishment of a remarkable coalition of agrarian interests, which saw graziers and landless labourers, previously bitter enemies, fighting together in the struggle against landlordism. Ultimately, of course, such a coalition could not be sustained and, in time, a powerful new rural elite comprising the graziers and strong farmers would emerge as the key voice in rural Ireland. The immediate priority for the graziers was a reduction in rent, but the obvious land hunger among the landless and smallholders, particularly in the west, was certain to increase the demand for the break-up of the large grazing ranches. Yet during the brief period that the coalition held together, the Land League, by directing its fire at the institution of landlordism, which became synonymous with British rule, politicised rural Catholic Ireland more effectively than any previous movement. This success was due to the raising of self-reliance among the tenant farmers and to the League's ability to give economic factors a political dimension. While it instilled the belief in the Irish farmer's mind that he had the right to own his land, the League was also regarded as a demonstration of resistance to British rule in Ireland.

In general, the Catholic Church was slow to respond to the appearance of the Land League. The hierarchy was naturally wary of identifying with any movement that had such obvious links with the Fenians, but the lower clergy were often sympathetic. In the autumn of 1879 parish priests in

Mayo began to join the League, and Archbishop Croke's tacit support for its objectives probably encouraged the spread of the Land League beyond its Mayo base. As the League developed, the lower clergy became more prominent, and new branches were based on the parish structure. The main weapons of the League were propaganda and intimidation, not violence, and the provincial press was solidly behind the new movement. Undoubtedly, increased literacy rates played their part in spreading the League's message. While the Land League was an open and legal organisation, frequently stressing the use of non-violent methods and a commitment to moral force, its leaders, both at local and national level, understood the value of violence. Beginning in the west, violence became widespread, but was never endemic. It did, of course, attract a huge amount of publicity but, measured against the level of agrarian protest, the violence was restrained. Moreover, agrarian crime was very much local in character and was often a response to local economic factors. In 1878, the rate of evictions over the whole country doubled from the previous year, and this figure continued to rise before reaching a peak in the spring of 1882. Not surprisingly, there was a close correlation between evictions and local agitation. Over the course of the Land War 67 murders were committed. Only a handful of these were landlords, land agents or others acting in the landed interest. Of the others, it seems that many of the killings were the result of local disputes in which the guilty parties used the cover of agrarian unrest to settle old scores. In truth, violence was effective during the Land War, because it was sufficient to ensure that intimidation, the League's key weapon, had the desired outcome. This was widely successful in the application of the boycott, a campaign of social ostracism mounted against selected individuals and backed by the threat of violence. Indeed, it was this combination of moral and physical force that made the League's prosecution of the Land War so effective. Though motivated by local economic concerns, violence became political in character. It was condoned not just by militant agrarians such as Davitt, but by Parnell and his followers in the Home Rule party, who viewed it as tactical. In this way the Land War contributed to the culture of violence and rejection of authority, which was to be a feature of rural society for successive generations of nationalists. Above all, however, the land agitation witnessed widespread participation at grass roots level, and tactics such as the boycott were all the more effective because they were based on unity and collective action.

In this way the Land League developed as a mass movement able to channel the energy and enthusiasm released by the agrarian agitation into an effective strategy. Its meetings, usually held on Sundays, drew large crowds and, while a carnival atmosphere usually existed, those who attended were conscious of the fact that they were engaged in the defiance of authority. In essence, the League was about confrontation, and the target was British state power, not just the local landlord. Much of its success was due to its ability to mobilise the entire rural population on the land issue. To those attending the Sunday rallies, and this included RIC observers as well as Land League supporters, the prominent role played by local IRB activists in the organisation of the events was obvious. Their influence on posters advertising these demonstrations was equally noticeable. These posters frequently made a direct connection between the land question and national independence. Many of the Fenians who were drawn to the new movement were keen to exploit popular grievances in the hope that this would ultimately produce more widespread support for their revolutionary designs.

The fact that violence was restrained also encouraged the participation of the Catholic clergy. Indeed, the open involvement of the Fenian element at both local and national level acted as a spur to the Catholic Church, which was anxious to provide a counterbalance to possible Fenian extremism. Of equal importance to the Fenian contribution, of course, was the involvement in the land issue of Home Rule politicians eager to make political capital out of agrarian discontent. These men engaged with the masses in a direct way and, in the process, Irish nationalism, previously the complex preserve of the educated middle classes, became open and relevant for the great mass of people in the country. It was the timely appearance of this inspirational and dynamic political leadership that transformed the impressive mobilisation of rural Ireland into the kernel of a powerful nationalist movement. With all these groups on board, the Land League allowed Catholic Ireland to present a much more sharply defined version of nationality than anything that had been possible in the O'Connell era. At the same time, land and nationalism became inextricably bound together in the last quarter of the nineteenth century.

If the Land League was to fight evictions and support evicted tenants, it needed money. Consequently, in December 1879, Parnell travelled to America on a fund-raising mission, collecting a sum of £30,000 within two months. This provided the League with a solid financial footing and enabled it to appoint full-time organisers to coordinate the agitation. News of an impending general election in April 1880 brought Parnell back to Ireland, and he intended to use the campaign to strengthen his grip on the Home Rule party. His chief rival was William Shaw, who had acted as party chairman following Butt's death, but, by May 1880, Parnell had defeated the moderate Shaw in a leadership election by 23 votes to 18. The bedrock of Parnell's support was in Connacht, a testament to the Land League's strength in the west, and the majority of new MPs were firmly behind Parnell's leadership. Among the new intake of MPs was John Dillon, the son of the Young Irelander John Blake Dillon. Dillon, who had accompanied Parnell on his American tour, was one of a new breed of Home Rule politicians. A militant agrarian and very able organiser who established a network of contacts all over Ireland, Dillon and his young radical colleagues provided the necessary dynamic leadership on the ground which contributed to the League's spectacular growth. The accompanying agitation and the defiance of the Land League demanded a response from the government. A carrot-and-stick policy, combining conciliation and coercion, was the favoured option of Gladstone's Liberal government. Gladstone's early impression of the Parnellite movement was that it was not really representative of nationalist Ireland, and this partially explains his support for coercion. Coercive legislation came into force in the early part of 1881 and this led to the arrest of a number of prominent land agitators. Parnell and his followers provided fierce opposition to the Coercion Bill, and they were ejected from the House of Commons, when they caused uproar by vigorously protesting against Davitt's arrest. Reports of the chaotic scenes at Westminster drew appreciation among Parnell's supporters in Ireland, and the experience helped to forge the Home Rule party into a more cohesive force in Parliament. Yet Parnell now faced a dilemma. He had a choice to make between withdrawing to Ireland and staking all on further agitation, or working the constitutional process and building up support in Parliament. To the dismay of the militant agrarians, he chose the constitutional path. Indeed, a number of advanced nationalists in both the IRB and the Land League had already expressed disquiet over the direction that Parnell was taking the movement. They were particularly unhappy about the cult of personality that was developing around the leader, which later manifested itself as Parnellism.

The government's coercion tactics failed to stem the unrest in Ireland, but Gladstone unveiled the conciliation element in his Irish policy when he introduced a new Land Bill in 1881. Parnell's constitutional approach appeared to have paid rapid dividends. Gladstone's bill became law in August, and it finally granted the three Fs – fair rent, free sale and fixity of tenure. This was a major piece of legislation because it established the basis for a new relationship between landlord and tenant, ultimately easing the transition towards peasant ownership. The act established a Land Commission, which was granted the authority to adjudicate on rents and to advance up to 75 per cent of the purchase price of a tenant's holding if there was agreement to sell. In a sense this created a system of dual ownership in Ireland. Of course, the balance still lay with the landlords, but it seemed to them that Parnell and the Land League had forced intolerable concessions on a weak government. For the more radical agrarians, however, the 1881 Land Act was woefully inadequate, and Parnell criticised the legislation in his attempt to hold his agrarian coalition together.

At the same time, Parnell recognised the significance of the concessions granted by the government and he persuaded the Land League to "test the act", arguing that this was the best way to expose its limitations. Although his privately held views were much more moderate, Parnell was anxious to maintain the League's momentum, and he deliberately resorted to violent language to denounce the Land Act. Fortunately for his immediate political future, the government reacted to his intemperate outbursts by arresting him in October 1881, thereby shielding him from the consequences of a Land League split. With Parnell and many of the other leaders in Kilmainham jail, a new burst of agrarian unrest was unleashed. From his prison cell Parnell, bowing to pressure from his colleagues, issued an ill-judged 'No Rent' manifesto on 18 October, urging the tenants to withhold rent payments. As a result, the Land League was suppressed and, as Parnell had predicted, the manifesto proved to be a flop. In effect, the Land Act, in providing assistance to the more prosperous tenant farmers, opened up a serious division among the rural population, which the League had been struggling to contain.

Naturally, Parnell's imprisonment had inflamed the situation in rural Ireland, particularly in Connacht, but the main reason for the steep rise in violence was the reaction of the poorer tenant farmers who fell outside the scope of Gladstone's Land Act. Between October 1880 and April 1882 almost 3,500 instances of agrarian crime were reported, as law and order broke down completely over many areas in the west of the country. On his arrest Parnell had predicted that 'Captain Moonlight' would take his place, but he quickly became alarmed at the scale of the violence and was anxious to see it halted. So was Gladstone, and this prompted him to broker a deal with Parnell. The result of this unofficial agreement was the 'Kilmainham Treaty'. Parnell was released on 2 May 1882, giving vague assurances about using his influence to calm the situation in the Irish countryside and offering only general support for the Liberal government's progressive measures. In return, the government promised to drop coercion and make arrangements to have rent arrears wiped out. Soon, an Arrears Act provided £800,000 worth of relief for approximately 130,000 tenants who had fallen behind with their rents. Before this, however, the brutal murder in Dublin's Phoenix Park of the new Chief Secretary, Lord Frederick Cavendish, and his Under-Secretary, TH Burke, only four days after Parnell's release from Kilmainham, shocked opinion in Britain and Ireland. The Invincibles, a secret group of violent nationalists who had broken away from the Fenian movement, had carried out the attack. Parnell was stunned by the murders and even considered withdrawing from politics. A new coercion measure followed and all shades of nationalism were attacked in the English press. In Ireland itself widespread revulsion was a common reaction to the Phoenix Park atrocity, and Parnell was more determined than ever to bring all agitation to an end and focus nationalist energy on his political agenda. This was facilitated by the impact of the Arrears Act, which had done much to calm the situation in the agrarian heartlands, and by the economic upswing as agricultural prices gradually recovered. The Phoenix Park atrocity had also horrified Michael Davitt. While he was furious at what he regarded as Parnell's counter-revolutionary strategy, the murders meant that Davitt subsequently recoiled from rhetoric that might be seen as condoning violence in any form. With Davitt's position much weaker, Parnell's intention to pursue a more moderate, constitutional line encountered little opposition.

The Land League had served its purpose and was not revived. Indeed, it was possible that in the longer-term the League would have been fatally damaged by the impact of the 1881 Land Act. In its place Parnell established the Irish National League in October 1882, but its aims were clearly more political in character, with emphasis being laid on the advancement of the Home Rule cause. Although it was a highly centralised organisation, which gave less scope to grass roots activists, it continued and developed the work done by the Land League in raising political consciousness across nationalist Ireland. It was also very much under Parnell's control, and a measure of his personal popularity and recognised authority can be gauged from the £37,000 raised by the National League and handed over to the Irish leader. A heavily indebted Parnell welcomed this, and the collection was reminiscent of the gratitude once shown to O'Connell for his contribution to Irish nationalism. Again, the National League was able to swallow the Land League's structures at local level, and it soon had branches all over Ireland. From 1883 to 1885 the land question became subordinated to the national question as local grievances were increasingly linked to the demand for self-government. Moreover, the principle of Home Rule, hitherto a rather vague concept in rural Ireland, became more attractive as the belief took hold that only an Irish parliament could fully understand Irish problems.

While Parnell kept a firm grip on the reins of power, he allowed his able young lieutenants, who had demonstrated their leadership abilities during the Land War, a good measure of freedom, and they worked energetically to establish a new political momentum at local level. At the same time, the social composition of the Home Rule party was changing. Farmers and shopkeepers were becoming more prominent, and this trend was highlighted by the 1885 general election in which the number of petty bourgeois representatives rose sharply. There was also a significant increase in the number of Catholic Home Rulers. The church had overcome its early misgivings about endorsing a Protestant leader and threw its considerable weight behind the campaign for Home Rule, which it accepted was the best way to advance its own claims and satisfy the needs of its flock. The Home Rule party, or Irish Parliamentary Party (IPP) as it was often known, developed rapidly into a highly disciplined and effective political instrument. Its MPs were paid out of party funds and the 'parliamentary pledge', introduced in 1884, committed all Home Rule MPs to vote together on all occasions when the majority decided that the party should act in unison. The move to instil rigid discipline among the Irish MPs at Westminster came as a result of an initiative by Tim Healy who had been elected in 1880. A leading figure at the Irish bar, Healy grasped the importance of concerted action to maximise the influence of the Home Rule party in the House of

Commons, and he drafted the parliamentary pledge in August 1884. Two further developments strengthened Parnell's party. The 1884 Reform Act more than trebled the number of Irish men eligible to vote, from 220,000 to over 700,000. Most of the new voters were small tenant farmers, thereby solidifying the IPP's social base. This was augmented by the Redistribution Act of 1885 which reduced the representation of the boroughs.

A demonstration of the power that a disciplined Home Rule party could bring to bear at Westminster came in June 1885, when the IPP joined with the Conservatives to turn the Liberal government out of office. Parnell had been unhappy at Gladstone's reluctance to embrace Home Rule, and his action had demonstrated that the IPP could make or break governments at Westminster if the political arithmetic allowed. Although the minority Conservative administration quickly introduced an imaginative land purchase measure, which set a pattern for future land reform, the Prime Minster, Lord Salisbury, was not prepared to risk major political changes which, he was certain, would throw his own party into crisis. Indeed, the failure of the two great Westminster parties to agree on a bipartisan approach to Ireland created further opportunities for Parnell, who had clearly been successful in forcing the Irish question to the top of the political agenda in London. In the general election of 1885, the IPP, with its 86 seats, held the balance of power, as the Conservatives won 249 seats to the Liberals' 335 seats. Still frustrated by the Liberals' rejection of his Home Rule demand, Parnell had used his influence during the election campaign to persuade Irish voters in Britain to support Conservative candidates. Undoubtedly, this cost the Liberals a number of seats and strengthened Parnell's hand in the new Parliament. In view of the Conservative party's subsequent passionate defence of the Union, Parnell's actions may appear self-defeating, but the political reality in 1885 was that either of the two great Westminster parties could have taken up the Home Rule cause in order to wrong-foot their opponents. Indeed, it was probably true that Parnell, with his conservative instincts, may have preferred to reach an accommodation with the Conservative party on the Home Rule issue, but Salisbury's caution rendered such a step unlikely. The 1885 general election also proved to be a defining moment in Irish politics, sketching, as it did, a new political landscape, which would remain largely unaltered until 1918. Nationalism was now the dominant force in Ireland. The Liberal party had been decimated, and the Conservatives had retreated into their Ulster strongholds.

Both parties at Westminster recognised that a response to this development could not be avoided. Parnell had made the IPP a force at Westminster and Home Rule was now a live issue. He had squeezed land reforms from both main parties, but this had merely whetted his supporters' desire for further concessions. Parnellism reflected this growing Irish self-confidence. It had been built on solid agrarian foundations as the land issue had politicised the masses. Although he himself was a good landlord with a genuine sympathy for the peasantry, Parnell knew how to exploit the landlord-tenant conflict in order to advance his own political agenda. The land agitation was simply a means to an end, and it allowed him to win control of the political movement as he concentrated on parliamentary activity and the struggle for Home Rule. While nationalism was clearly rooted in the Irish soil and was the political creed of the dominant tenant farming class, the main theatre of activity, as far as Parnell was concerned, was Westminster. Unquestionably, he was a unifying force, carrying with him moderate nationalists, radical agrarians and constitutional Fenians. During 1885, Parnell's speeches and actions enabled him to cultivate his radical image. Both the famous Cork speech in January 1885, in which he suggested that complete separation rather than simple devolution was his ultimate goal, and his subsequent opposition to a royal visit to Ireland a few months later attracted Fenians to the National League. Furthermore, John O'Leary, the IRB leader since the death of Charles Kickham in 1882, ordered that nothing should be done to undermine Parnell's leadership. This allowed him to control his extremist followers and benefit from their support. Moreover, his National League, like the earlier Land League, was also successful in pulling together the various elements in Irish society. This coalition of rural and urban, prosperous farmer and landless labourer, gave Parnellism its mass following. This was consolidated by the leader's charisma and the deference shown by his key followers.

But, as the historian Paul Bew has pointed out, Parnell had another project. His aim was to find a compromise that would end the conflict between landlord and tenant. If accomplished, this would allow a reformed landlord class to join with him in the struggle for Home Rule and, thereby, enhance its prospects of success. The Irish leader clearly assumed that a demand for self-government brought forward by a Home Rule party, which included a significant number of landlords in its ranks, would receive a much more sympathetic hearing in Parliament. Parnell's view of his fellow landlords was obviously naive, but he was astute enough to realise that the tenant farmers' ultimate aim was to own their holdings. More radical alternatives, such as Davitt's plans for 'Land Nationalisation', were largely ignored, and this made the movement more conservative and in tune with Parnell and, therefore, easier to control. Of course, this chimed with the interests of the new rural elite of publicans, shopkeepers and graziers who now carried most political influence. Parnell also recognised that his political movement would be Catholic, and he had been careful to ensure that his speeches did not alienate the Catholic Church. By isolating Davitt and the radicals, Parnell also made it easier for the church to play a full part in Home Rule politics. In particular, the rules adopted by the National League for the selection of prospective parliamentary candidates were framed in a manner that ensured conservative control of the county conventions in which the clergy frequently played a leading role. On a national level, of course, Parnell retained complete control over the organisation's executive.

In this way the parallels between O'Connellism and Parnellism were strengthened though, of course, essential differences remained. As was the case with O'Connell and repeal, Parnell never offered a precise definition of Home Rule, nor did he commit himself to give a clear undertaking that Home Rule should be regarded as a final constitutional settlement. This left Home Rule as a catch-all ideology, which could hold the support of all shades of nationalist opinion. Moreover, both O'Connell and Parnell could link militant rhetoric to the pragmatic pursuit of attainable objectives. Still, the dramatic improvement in communications in the second half of the nineteenth century, principally through the development of the railways, meant that Parnellism had a wider geographical reach than O'Connellism. Its real strength had been in Leinster and Munster. Furthermore, O'Connell was much more a man of the people in the sense that he had direct contact with his followers, whereas Parnell was obviously a more remote figure, relying on the press to communicate with his supporters. He was, however, much less dependent on the Catholic Church.

Parnellism received a further boost with the bizarre events of December 1885, when news was leaked that Gladstone was now in favour of Home Rule. Clearly, Parnellism had also influenced the great Liberal leader, though recent historical research has questioned the speed of his conversion, suggesting that Gladstone had been considering Irish Home Rule from the mid-1870s. In some speeches on the Irish Question in 1882 and 1883 he had been careful not to dismiss Home Rule out of hand. Instead, Gladstone had dwelt on the practical difficulties of devolving power to Ireland. In fact, he was prepared to consider a variety of reforms for Ireland, including Home Rule, which he judged would preserve the Union. This was his primary concern. Back in government, Gladstone began preparations for the Home Rule Bill, which was introduced in April 1886. Previously, the essential core of Parnellism had been the pragmatism of a highly disciplined IPP, which acted independently of the great English parties in order to force concessions from both of them. By temperament, it seems that Parnell would have preferred to work with the Conservative party, but news of Gladstone's dramatic conversion nudged him into an alliance with the Liberals. While this may have been the only practical course open to the Irish leader, it rendered Parnellism less effective. On the surface, Home Rule meant simply giving a new Irish parliament control over domestic affairs, but this masks the complex nature of the financial and constitutional arrangements deemed necessary for the smooth working of this devolution experiment. For both Gladstone and Parnell, moreover, Home Rule had to be accompanied by the introduction of a comprehensive land purchase scheme, which would reconcile the landlord class and allow its members to assume a prominent role in any new devolved parliament.

The combined support of IPP and Liberal MPs should have guaranteed the Home Rule Bill's passage in the House of Commons, but, in the event, the measure was defeated by 343 votes to 313. The Liberal party had split on the issue, with 93 Liberal MPs voting against Home Rule. Gladstone had been deserted by the party's old Whig element, which shared Conservative fears that Home Rule would cause long-term damage to the Empire. More significantly, a large group of radical Liberals led by Joseph Chamberlain was fiercely opposed to Gladstone's new Irish strategy, even though Chamberlain was known to favour some form of autonomy for Ireland. Chamberlain was adamant that Home Rule would destroy the Union, warning that it would never satisfy Irish nationalists who, he claimed, would continue to demand incremental progress towards complete separation. Indeed, some of Parnell's speeches, including his celebrated Cork speech, had warned that "no man has the right to fix the boundary to the march of a nation", suggesting that Home Rule would be viewed as a first instalment rather than a final settlement. Of course, Parnell's own views were more moderate than his public statements. Such rhetoric had the two-fold purpose of laying down a marker for future negotiations and maintaining unity among the various factions supporting Parnell. But the influential Chamberlain had raised another objection to Home Rule. He argued that public opinion in Britain would not accept the abandonment of fellow Anglo-Saxon Protestants living in Ulster, but both Gladstone and Parnell played down the threat that Ulster posed to Home Rule. Although the details of the Home Rule Bill of 1886 seem fairly innocuous, as the powers granted to the new Irish parliament were strictly limited, the passions aroused by the proposals were unprecedented. In the end, the issue was settled by the defection of so many Liberals, but the arguments would be repeated over the next 30 years.

Two days after the Home Rule Bill's defeat Parliament was dissolved, but Gladstone's appeal to the electorate on the issue was firmly rejected. In the general election of July 1886 the Conservatives won a landslide victory, as the Liberals were reduced to only 191 seats. The IPP repeated its success of the previous year but, with the new Conservative government expressing outright opposition to Irish self-government, Parnell had little room to manoeuvre. He had come close to bringing off a spectacular triumph, but the prospects for the future success of Home Rule now clearly depended on the future prospects for Gladstone's Liberal party. For Parnell, the old strategy of independent action at Westminster was no longer an option. Closer cooperation with the Liberals had to be developed, and Parnell recognised that any renewal of agrarian agitation might place an intolerable strain on the Liberal alliance. Yet most indicators pointed to a renewal of the Land War in the autumn of 1886. A downturn in agricultural prices, which began in 1885 and continued into 1886, brought more hardship to the tenant farmers. Moreover, the political vacuum created by the defeat of the Home Rule Bill encouraged Parnell's more militant followers to return to land agitation. These men regarded agrarian agitation as an assertion of their nationalist rights, and were convinced that a combination of political action and agrarian agitation was the best way to advance the nationalist cause.

The two most prominent radical agrarians, John Dillon and William O'Brien, were responsible for directing the Plan of Campaign, the title given to the new phase of the Land War, which was launched in October 1886. The essence of the Plan was to target individual estates and offer these landlords a reduced rent. If this was refused, the money was paid into an estate fund, which was used to compensate individual tenants who faced eviction as a consequence of their actions. The operation of the Plan was confined to approximately 200 estates, most of which had been selected because the landlord was known to be in financial difficulty and was, therefore, more susceptible to pressure. In many ways the economic crisis was deeper than in the previous decade, but, though the new agitation was brilliantly organised, it failed to present an effective challenge to landlordism. Again, most of the activity took place in the south and west, where tenant distress was most acute. Physical violence, intimidation and the boycott also resurfaced, but the Plan never enjoyed the success achieved by the Land League and suffered from lack of funds. Unlike the Land War, the Plan was not supported by money from America, and it could not gather a similar coalition of rural interests or generate anything approaching the agrarian dynamism of the 1879–82 period. By the end of 1890 the agitation had petered out in the face of resolute action taken by Salisbury's Conservative government, which developed a tough security policy to combat the agitation. While this served the government's immediate purpose and, incidentally, paved the way for a series of imaginative Conservative reforms in Ireland, participation in the conflict had, once again, strengthened the unity of purpose within nationalist ranks. The land question, therefore, retained the ability to transform Irish nationalism into a united and cohesive force.

Parnell did not support the new wave of agitation associated with the Plan. Indeed, as early as December 1886, he had sought to restrain Dillon and O'Brien and curb the level of agitation. Whereas Parnell's radical lieutenants believed that a renewal of the land agitation was necessary to maintain nationalist momentum, their leader was concerned about the problems that widespread agitation would create for the Liberal alliance. He was adamant that the land issue had served its purpose, and he played no part in the implementation of the Plan. In the late 1880s Parnell's primary focus was on the political aim of Home Rule, and he became much more concerned with English, rather than Irish, public opinion. During the late 1880s he consistently sought to reassure the Liberals that Home Rule would be a positive move for Britain and the Empire. In particular, Parnell argued that a Home Rule parliament in Dublin, dealing only with domestic issues, was the limit of his aspirations, but he also endorsed Gladstone's view that a Home Rule settlement for Ireland would actually strengthen the Union. By this stage, moreover, Irish nationalists shared many of the values of popular liberalism. For an increasing number of Liberal MPs Home Rule was equated with reform and judged to be the only alternative to repression, which these same Liberal backbenchers were so quick to condemn in other European countries.

But Parnell had more personal reasons for his refusal to become embroiled in the Irish land question at this point. In 1880 he had begun a liaison with Katherine O'Shea, the wife of one of his parliamentary colleagues and, by 1886, the couple were living together in Eltham, south-east London. Spending most of his time with Mrs O'Shea, Parnell, who often suffered from ill-health, neglected his role as IPP leader at Westminster and actually only visited Ireland once in the period 1886–90, leaving others to promote the nationalist cause at home. Parnell had always been cold and aloof with his Irish colleagues, but his frequent absences now undermined his authority. This relationship with Mrs O'Shea was an open secret. Many of Parnell's political associates were aware of the relationship, and Katherine's estranged husband, Captain William O'Shea, not only connived at the affair but also sought to exploit it for his own political advancement. Indeed, Parnell had pulled more than a few strings to have Captain O'Shea adopted as the IPP candidate in the Galway City by-election in February 1886. Opposition to O'Shea's selection was led by the outraged Healy, a key figure in the IPP, who never forgave Parnell for his uncompromising tactics in the selection procedure. O'Shea had not taken the parliamentary pledge, and he actually refused to support the Home Rule Bill only four months after his election. Following this dramatic twist, O'Shea resigned his seat, knowing that he could expect no further political favours from Parnell. Yet the Irish leader also knew that it was only the prospect of a sizeable bequest from Katherine's ageing aunt that prevented O'Shea from initiating divorce proceedings. This situation was unlikely to continue, and Parnell must have been aware of the threat that a messy divorce case might pose to his political future.

Still, all this lay ahead. Before the divorce case shocked Victorian Britain, Parnell was involved in another legal tangle, which enhanced his reputation on the mainland. In 1887, *The Times* ran a series of articles under the heading 'Parnellism and Crime', alleging that Parnell and his party had been involved in criminal acts. The articles were based on letters, supposedly written by Parnell, the most damaging of which expressed the Irish leader's regret in having to condemn the Phoenix Park murders. The Conservative government hoped to expose Parnell's murky past by establishing a special commission to investigate the charges, but the plan backfired when, in February 1889, the letters were found to be forgeries.

This dramatic news raised Parnell's stature to new heights, particularly in England, but, in December 1889, six months after the death of Katherine's rich aunt, an angry O'Shea, who had been passed over in the will, filed a petition for divorce, citing Parnell as co-respondent. Before the case came to court in November 1890, Parnell had assured his associates that his career would not suffer, but the details that emerged in court cast Parnell in a squalid light. Despite the revelations, the IPP nervously gave him their unanimous backing. Within a week, however, the situation had been reversed once it became known that the Liberal party, which contained a powerful nonconformist wing, would not, in spite of Gladstone's efforts, continue in alliance with the IPP while Parnell remained as leader. On 6 December 1890 the Home Rule MPs, meeting in the House of Commons, faced the agonising dilemma of choosing between Home Rule and Parnell. Amid bitter acrimony they chose Home Rule, and Parnell was deposed as leader. Immediately, the party split into two unequal factions, with the minority remaining loyal to Parnell. If the 'Chief' was unnerved by this sequence of events, he did not show it. Parnell gave notice that he would battle for his reinstatement and decided to take the fight to Ireland, declaring that he owed his position as leader to the people of Ireland, not to his fellow Irish MPs. The episode had also demonstrated that Parnell's political strategy after 1886 had weakened his authority in both the party and the country, while his autocratic style of leadership had created a number of bitter personal enemies who now sought revenge.

Parnell was given a rapturous welcome on his return to Dublin, but it soon emerged that he would face insurmountable opposition in Ireland. The Catholic Church, which had maintained a low profile during the divorce proceedings, finally came off the fence as the hierarchy switched sides and denounced the former leader. Earlier, the church had overcome its initial hesitation by identifying closely with a political movement that had a Protestant as its leader. For his part, Parnell had always been careful not to alienate the Catholic Church through his public statements. A more formal alliance between the church and the IPP had existed since October 1884, when the hierarchy had asked the party to represent Catholic educational interests in Parliament. In the weeks immediately following the revelations concerning Parnell's personal life, the church was very reluctant to issue any kind of condemnation, preferring to leave the issue to the members of the IPP. It certainly appeared that the church lacked the confidence to seize the initiative and feared that it would be accused of interfering in politics. When the Catholic bishops finally took the plunge in attacking Parnell, however, they exerted a powerful influence on the outcome of electoral contests in Ireland, particularly in the 1892 general election.

Of course, a good part of Parnell's legacy was based on his heroic struggle against impossible odds in the final nine months of his life. During this period Parnell demonstrated that his political skills had not been diminished by his self-imposed exile, and his performance was, at times, reminiscent of the heady days of 1879–81, when he had pushed constitutionalism to its limits. However, his failure to rally the people was confirmed by crushing defeats for Parnell's candidates in three crucial by-elections, when the influence of the church proved decisive. During these campaigns Parnell seized every opportunity to attack his opponents, but it was clear that he was becoming increasingly desperate. He appealed directly to 'the hillside men', as he sought electoral support from Fenian sympathisers who had backed him in his early career. These violent speeches were an indication of Parnell's profound sense of despair rather than a change of political direction. Parnell never abandoned constitutional politics, and he retained sufficient vision to warn of the dangers inherent in narrow sectarian nationalism, arguing that the Catholic majority in Ireland needed to adopt a more conciliatory, accommodating attitude towards their fellow Irishmen. Yet such was the bitter feeling aroused by the leadership struggle that this kind of perceptive analysis was lost among the personal invective.

The exertions of Parnell's Irish campaign had taken its toll on his health, and he died in October 1891 following a short illness. His funeral in Dublin drew a crowd estimated at 200,000, as a shocked Ireland had to come to terms with his tragic and premature death. A testament to Parnell's great ability to unite all shades of nationalism was the way in which he came to be regarded as an inspiration to both constitutional and revolutionary nationalists. Parnell's impact at Westminster had forced English politicians to look at Ireland in a new light, as Home Rule and land reform became central issues in British politics. Both his followers and his opponents had seen how a united, disciplined party could exploit differences at Westminster to Ireland's advantage. Parnell had made Home Rule for Ireland realpolitik, and his influence was felt well outside Irish politics. While the Fenians regarded the 1886 Home Rule Bill as a miserable concession, Parnell's ability to generate excitement in all nationalist ranks guaranteed Fenian support during the critical period of tenant farmer mobilisation. Looking back, these Fenians built up the image of a leader whose real political aspirations had been thwarted by the conservative forces at the heart of Irish nationalism, which reflected the views of Ireland's rural Catholic bourgeoisie. This retrospective Fenian analysis was, of course, flawed, but it was true that Parnell, more than either Gladstone or his own nationalist colleagues, had recognised the need to make positive overtures to northern Protestants. His famous Ulster Hall speech in 1891 urged moderation, and probably only Michael Davitt among the leaders of nationalism, who was a regular visitor to Ulster, had as good an understanding of Ulster Protestant sensitivities on the Home Rule issue.

The leadership feud had done serious damage to constitutional nationalism, and the split continued with even greater bitterness after Parnell's death. In the general election of July 1892 the anti-Parnellites, as they had become known, won 71 seats, while the Parnellite group under John Redmond won only 9 seats. However, this rout of the Parnellites was not as complete as these figures suggest. Outside Ulster, Parnellite candidates had secured one-third of the votes cast, and they had polled particularly well in urban areas. Redmond blamed clerical influence for the Parnellites' poor showing in rural constituencies, but the key reason for the success of the anti-Parnellites was the electors' belief in the argument that only the maintenance of the Liberal alliance could deliver Home Rule. Redmond's call for a return to independent opposition at Westminster was rejected, and the anti-Parnellites appeared to be vindicated when a second Home Rule Bill was introduced in February 1893. The general election of the previous year had returned Gladstone and the Liberals to government and, once again, the Irish party held the balance of power. Although his party remained nervous on the Home Rule issue, Gladstone's personal commitment was beyond question. Furthermore, at the end of a very long political career, the great Liberal leader was determined to bring peace to

Ireland and regarded Home Rule both as unfinished business and a moral necessity. While he was, by this stage, more aware of Ulster opposition to any Home Rule scheme, he firmly rejected all demands for special treatment, and the main features of the 1886 Bill were retained. Every clause of the second Home Rule Bill was bitterly contested as the discussion process dragged on for 82 days, but Gladstone's nerve held and the measure was passed by a majority of 34 in the House of Commons. Irish nationalists were jubilant, but Gladstone had calculated that he needed a majority of 100 in order to force the Lords' hand on the issue. Even this was wishful thinking and, in September 1893, the House of Lords overwhelmingly rejected the second Home Rule Bill. Gladstone was ready to continue the struggle, but his party shared neither his vision nor his enthusiasm. In 1894 he retired from politics and the Liberal party put Home Rule on the back burner.

The IPP split had not helped Gladstone's efforts to sell Home Rule to his Liberal backbenchers. Indeed, Redmond, the Parnellite leader, had openly criticised certain aspects of the 1893 Bill, when many assumed that the measure would highlight the need for an end to division within nationalism. The split continued through the general election of July 1895, in which the anti-Parnellites won 70 seats, leaving Redmond's group with only 11 seats. The 1895 contest also revealed the increased political apathy in Ireland following the damage done by the Parnell split. Only 42 of the seats were contested, a figure which was down by 50 per cent on the 1892 level. The fact that Home Rule was off the agenda at Westminster naturally dampened enthusiasm, but there was also a sense of disgust among grass roots nationalists, who had been demoralised and embarrassed by the spectacle of the split and the subsequent petty squabbling among the various factions struggling for control. Constitutional nationalism had been discredited. While Redmond repeatedly charged his opponents with betrayal, there was, if anything, even greater division among the anti-Parnellite majority. On his removal as chairman of the Irish party in December 1890, Parnell had been replaced by Justin McCarthy. Though he was popular and highly regarded by many of his parliamentary colleagues, McCarthy had neither the authority nor the force of personality to maintain unity among the anti-Parnellite group of MPs. The two heavyweights in the movement were John Dillon and Tim Healy and, from the early days of the Home Rule movement, they had been highly suspicious of each other.

In addition to their bitter personal rivalry, however, there were significant ideological differences between the two.

Healy was from the clericalist right wing of the party. He wanted more power devolved to the constituencies, particularly in relation to the selection of candidates, where local priests would be in a position to exercise more influence. Moreover, Healy did not subscribe to the argument that the Liberal alliance should form the basis of IPP strategy. This put him at odds with Dillon. Though a devout Catholic, Dillon was consistent in his opposition to clerical participation in politics. Furthermore, he was determined to retain the powerful central authority that had been established by Parnell. This put Dillon and Healy on a collision course. Gladstone's retirement from politics in 1894 ensured that the Liberal party's enthusiasm for Home Rule would never reach its previous level, but Dillon clung to the belief that all the Irish party's efforts should be concentrated on securing Home Rule and that the only way to achieve this was by fostering the Liberal alliance.

Even the Conservative victory in the 1895 general election did not shake Dillon's confidence. By this stage the rivalry between the Dillonite and Healyite factions had burst into the open, as each side sought to have their supporters nominated for safe IPP seats. In the general election Dillon enjoyed a narrow advantage, and he was determined to press this home in the immediate post-election period. Matters came to a head, when a by-election was held in South Kerry in September 1895. Healy had moved quickly to persuade local clergy in the constituency to endorse the candidature of one of his closest supporters, but Dillon insisted that an 'official party' candidate should contest the seat. After an extremely bitter campaign Dillon's nominee was declared the victor. In February 1896 Dillon replaced McCarthy as party chairman, and he would use his new role to expel Healy and his supporters, whom he accused of disloyalty and insubordination, from positions of influence within the party's organisation. Although this had been achieved by the end of 1896, Healy continued to enjoy a measure of support within nationalist circles. In January 1897, with considerable clerical support, Healy launched the People's Rights Association as a rival to the National Federation, the Irish party's organisation, but his efforts to create a conservative Catholic party and, simultaneously, to undermine Dillon met with failure.

Dillon had won the power struggle, but the faction fighting of the

1890s had discredited constitutional nationalism. The constant sniping between the Redmondites, the Healyites and the Dillonites in the mid-1890s provided a sharp contrast to the unity and cohesion established by Parnell during the early 1880s. Moreover, the land issue was no longer the dynamic economic factor that had energised Irish nationalism. Successive Conservative governments, beginning in 1885, had sought to remove the land question from the nationalist equation. In a sense, therefore, Lord Salisbury's Conservative government was acknowledging that the land question and the national question were inseparable. Based on the principle of land purchase, the Treasury provided funds to compensate landlords and allow tenants to purchase their holdings. Dillon was suspicious of Conservative intentions, believing that land purchase might, as the Conservatives themselves hoped, dilute Irish nationalism and, thereby, dampen the demand for Home Rule. Initially, these government subsidies were given a lukewarm reception by Irish tenants, who considered the financial terms imposed by the state to be unattractive. The Conservative government was moving in the right direction, but it would take the generous terms offered by the 1903 Wyndham Act to achieve the overhaul of land tenure which, ultimately, the state, the landlords and the tenants desired.

Before this, however, the land question, once again, demonstrated its capacity to mobilise the tenant farming class. A new wave of agrarian agitation broke out in Connacht in 1896, as the familiar pattern of poor harvests and economic hardship returned. The key figure in channelling the new agrarian protest movement was William O'Brien, who had established his credentials as an agrarian campaigner during the days of the Land League and the Plan of Campaign. O'Brien had been a close associate of Dillon's, but he had retired as an MP in 1895, dismayed by the Irish party's failure to resolve its differences. Settling in County Mayo, O'Brien was immediately struck by the suffering of the Connacht smallholders. He then witnessed, at first hand, the impact of the failure of the potato crop in 1896 and 1897 and the fear of a new famine. Initially, O'Brien assumed that it would take a reunited Irish party under Dillon's leadership to direct the agitation but, when his efforts to draw the warring factions together were frustrated, O'Brien turned away from his former parliamentary colleagues and looked to grass roots activists in Connacht. Dillon was suspicious of O'Brien's plans, believing that once the land problem was settled tenant farmers would no longer support the parliamentary campaign for Home Rule, and he, therefore, refused to participate in this new phase of agrarian politics.

On 23 January 1898, at a public gathering in Westport, O'Brien launched the United Irish League (UIL). Through the new movement O'Brien sought to channel the agitation, which, naturally, saw a return to the successful tactics used by the Land League. Indeed, many historians take the view that the Land War can best be understood as a conflict which ran from 1879, and the birth of the Land League, to 1903, and the Wyndham Act, with the UIL dominating the final phase of the agitation. Unlike the previous campaigns, when the Protestant landlord was the target of the agitation, the UIL focused its attention on local Catholic graziers. Initially, the church opposed the new movement, but, as the UIL became established, the clergy realised that only through participation could they hope to moderate the UIL's more radical policies. In raising the cry of "the land for the people", O'Brien was demanding the break-up of both the estates and the grazing ranches. Significantly, the UIL also introduced the concept of compulsory purchase, which it regarded as the best way to achieve its aim of tenant ownership. Facing this new challenge of agrarian protest, the government responded in a predictable manner by turning to coercion. In the late 1890s, however, all the ingredients for successful agitation in the west were in place and, under O'Brien's brilliant, inspirational leadership, the UIL overcame government resistance. Although it never generated the popular enthusiasm of the early 1880s, O'Brien managed to mould spasmodic agrarian outrages into a coherent organisation that claimed over 50,000 members within two years of its formation.

But O'Brien also had a political motive in launching his agrarian movement, because he hoped to use the UIL to reunite the Irish party. In addition to reinvigorating Irish nationalism and maintaining pressure for reform, O'Brien believed that the land issue could provide the common ground to enable the various factions to work together. Yet, in seeking party unity, O'Brien came into conflict with his old colleague, Dillon, who feared that the new focus on agrarian activity would divert nationalist energy from the Home Rule struggle. Still, by the end of 1898, Dillon had recognised that the UIL would not go away, and he sought to make the best of the situation by agreeing that the UIL should replace the National Federation as the party's organisation. In spite of his lack of enthusiasm, it was clear that grass roots activity, or pressure from below, rather than Dillon's preference for high politics, was pushing the party towards reunion. Significantly, the League made a major impact in the local government elections of 1899 following the overhaul of local government in the previous year. Its performance transformed the UIL from a western agrarian movement into a national political organisation, demonstrating its capacity to mobilise popular nationalist support. Although O'Brien succeeded in using the UIL to unite Dillonites, Healyites and Redmondites, his hope that a reunited party would continue to press the League's agrarian programme was not fulfilled. In his effort to reunite the party O'Brien was aided by Dillon's resignation, made in a fit of pique, from the leadership of the anti-Parnellite group. This allowed him to secure agreement between Redmond and Healy. Thereafter, Dillon, fearing isolation and the further loss of influence, threw his support behind the reunion attempts. After nearly ten years of bitter feuding the IPP was formally reunited on 30 January 1900. Dillon had taken the decisive step of outlining a programme that provided the basis for unity. He advocated a return to the old party's constitution and declared that the reunited party would pursue an independent line at Westminster, where it would concentrate on securing Home Rule, but would also fight for social and economic reforms, which would be of benefit to Ireland. Crucially, Dillon bowed to pressure from O'Brien and, on 6 February 1900, Redmond was declared the unanimous choice to lead the reunited party. In June the UIL was formally integrated into the party and was officially accepted as the IPP's national organisation.

Although the party had been reunited under Redmond's chairmanship, it never recaptured the dynamism of the early Parnellite period. The land issue had breathed life into constitutional nationalism and transformed the IPP into a vibrant, dynamic movement, led by a charismatic personality. The party became a highly disciplined and effective political instrument, and it enjoyed a mass following in the country. This made constitutional nationalism an umbrella movement, drawing support from the various social strata in Catholic Ireland. Parnell had moved swiftly to control and contain his radical agrarian followers once this successful mobilisation had been achieved, but the split of 1890–91 brought many of these long-standing tensions to the surface.

In the last quarter of the nineteenth century the land and the national questions had become inseparable. All those involved in the agrarian movement were instinctive, if not political, nationalists. Home Rule remained their core ideological belief, based on the simple assumption that only an Irish administration could solve Irish problems. But this ignored Westminster's success in overcoming the land problem. Having established the principle of land purchase, it only remained for the government to put together a comprehensive package backed by generous funding to resolve the land question. Although agrarian agitation was revived spasmodically in the early years of the twentieth century, the 1903 Wyndham Act had achieved its purpose. It was the result of an agreement between landlord and tenant, appealing to the landlord by providing a 12 per cent bonus for the sale of an entire estate, and to the tenant by ensuring that annual repayments were lower than existing rents. This enabled the majority of tenant farmers to become owner-occupiers. Ultimately, the legislation also altered the relationship between land and nationalism, but this was not recognised by the IPP. Indeed, the land question had become so ingrained in Irish political culture that it continued to influence social and political relationships well into the twentieth century.

*1. Right:* William Pitt the Younger
(1759–1806), attributed to Thomas
Gainsborough

*2. Below:* Grattan's Parliament. The
Irish House of Commons by Francis
Wheatley.
Grattan stands at the front right, beside
the two seated figures, addressing the
House.

3. Daniel O'Connell (1775–1847)

4. Duke of Wellington (1769–1852)
by Francisco Goya

5. Robert Peel (1788–1850) by EA Duyckinick

6. *Left:* The Staff of the *Irish People* newspaper. From left to right: Denis Dowling Mulcahy, Thomas Clarke Luby and John O'Leary.

7. *Below left:* John O'Leary (1830–1907)

8. *Below right:* James Fintan Lalor (1807–1849)

JOHN O'LEARY

9. *Left:* James Stephens
(1824–1901)

*10. Right:* John Mitchel
(1815–1875)

11. *Above:* 'Trial of Mitchel', from Mitchel's Jail Journal, which was first serialised in his first New York newspaper, *The Citizen*, in 1854

12. *Below:* 'Trial of Robert Emmet', Emmet replying to the verdict of high treason, 19 September 1803

TRIAL OF ROBERT EMMET.

13. *Left:* Michael Davitt
(1846–1906)

14. *Right:* Charles
Stewart Parnell
(1846–1891)

15. William Ewart Gladstone (1809–1898)

16. *Left*: John Dillon
(1851–1927)

17. *Right*: William
O'Brien (1852–1928)

*18. Right:* John Redmond
(1856–1918)

*19. Left:* Lord
Salisbury
(1830–1903)

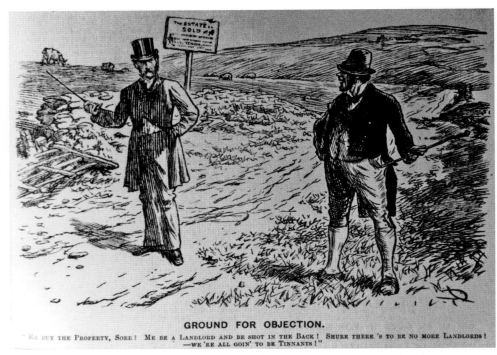

GROUND FOR OBJECTION.

"ME BUY THE PROPERTY, SORR! ME BE A LANDLORD AND BE SHOT IN THE BACK! SHURE THERE'S TO BE NO MORE LANDLORDS! —WE'RE ALL GOIN' TO BE TINNANTS!"

*20. Above:* 'Ground for Objection', *Punch Cartoon*, 14 May 1881

*21. Right:* 'The Rivals', *Punch Cartoon*, 13 August 1881

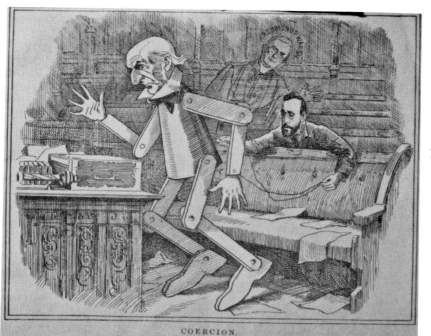

*22. Left:*
'Coercion'

COERCION.

He can talk by the yard, he can plot and can plan,
And Home Rule hymns can sing;
But where is the good of this Grand Old Man
If it's Healy that pulls the string?

AT THE CROSS ROADS.

Joe (the Cow-boy). "HOI!—*THIS* BE YOUR ROAD, MEASTER!"

*23. Above:* 'At the Crossroads', *Punch Cartoon*, 13 February 1886

*24. Left:* William
Butler Yeats
(1865–1939)

*25. Right:* Douglas
Hyde (1860–1949)

26. *Right:* Colonel Edward Saunderson (1837–1906)

27. *Left:* Horace Plunkett (1854–1932)

28. Sir Edward Carson (1854–1935)

# Chapter 5

# The Development of
# Cultural Nationalism

T HE UPHEAVAL WITHIN CONSTITUTIONAL nationalism during the 1890s
encouraged the growth of other forms of nationalism. The fallout from
the Parnell split had discredited the IPP, and something of a vacuum had
been created within Irish political life. Another factor encouraging new
developments within Irish nationalism was the realisation that corruption
had become embedded in the political life of nationalist Ireland. A
sophisticated patronage machine had emerged, particularly at local level
where local nationalist leaders often controlled jobs. Critics frequently
highlighted appointments made by the Local Government Board, which
had been formed in 1872, and pointed to the allocation of grants that
were made under the auspices of the Congested Districts Board, a body
established in 1891 by Arthur Balfour, the Conservative Chief Secretary, to
alleviate poverty in western counties. For others the essential pragmatism
and social conservatism of constitutional nationalism and parliamentary
politics failed to capture the imagination of a minority, which favoured
more discussion of ideas and political debate, rather than the personality
politics which tended to dominate after the IPP split.

Even as the UIL sought to bring an end to the internal feuding and unite
the party from below, urban intellectuals who scoffed at the League's narrow
agrarian agenda attacked it. Such people were drawn to cultural nationalism,
which was to develop as a significant force at the end of the nineteenth
century. Previously, constitutional nationalists had given little thought to
Ireland's cultural identity, but this was challenged by new thinking in Irish
intellectual circles that political nationalism had to be reinforced by a strong
cultural dimension if it was to meet with success. Parnell's dominance
and the aura of infallibility associated with the Chief had discouraged any

such deviation, but his removal and the hitherto concealed weakness of the IPP had clearly altered the situation. Moreover, European influences had suggested that the development of a cultural identity was a necessary prerequisite for the advance of political nationalism, and this oversight had to be belatedly addressed. Indeed, this view had been echoed previously by a number of Fenian thinkers who believed that there had to be much greater focus on the development of national consciousness to prepare the country and its people for political independence.

At another level the awakening of cultural nationalism can be viewed as a reaction to the modernisation of Irish society in the second half of the nineteenth century. Significantly, this critique of modernisation became entangled and confused with resistance to anglicisation, and this was to give cultural nationalism an added political dimension. The upheaval caused by the myriad of social and economic changes towards the end of the century had contributed to an identity crisis in Irish society and encouraged those affected to look backwards in search of their cultural and historical roots. It was also true that many of those first drawn to cultural nationalism, usually urban intellectuals, had, up to that point, shown little interest in political nationalism. They experienced a general feeling of insecurity, and they were uncomfortable with the remorseless advance of commercialisation. This brought them into conflict with political nationalism which had, of course, benefited from economic developments such as the spread of the railways and the rapid growth of newspapers. In fact, constitutional nationalists had sought to reflect such modernisation and, in their commitment to the Liberal alliance, leading figures such as Dillon identified wholeheartedly with the progressive social policies of British Liberalism.

It was also apparent that the upper echelon of the IPP, including the parliamentary party, was a closed shop, leaving a considerable section of the Catholic bourgeoisie frustrated by the lack of opportunity for those with political ambition. Instead, these younger, educated men and women were drawn to cultural nationalism, which provided an outlet for their political energy and allowed real opportunities for self-expression. Within these bourgeois ranks, of course, there was a collection of sub strata. At the top were business and professional people, and this continued through the proprietors of the provincial press, civil servants, schoolmasters, the clergy, shopkeepers and publicans in the towns and villages, many of whom had farming interests. Furthermore, the modernisation of Irish society had increased the numbers and importance of the educated lower middle class, the petty bourgeoisie, who took up positions as clerks, salesmen and shop assistants. Taken together, such people might be described as the respectable classes, and they were seeking social opportunities, and not simply political participation or advancement. The older generation, which had been blooded in the early days of the Land League, enjoyed a stranglehold on the party and its organisation at both local and national level. Frustrated by their exclusion and yet retaining political ambition, these younger petty bourgeois elements quickly became disillusioned with conventional politics and, not surprisingly, were also attracted to the opportunities presented by participation in the emerging cultural nationalist movement. These opportunities meant that there was now a forum for women to engage in cultural and political life. Earlier, the Ladies' Land League, under the leadership of Parnell's sister, Anna, had been formed in 1881. It had acted as a support organisation to the Land League, but it was quickly wound up, as Anna Parnell claimed that it had been undermined and isolated by the broader nationalist movement. Still, the Ladies' Land League had provided some experience for women who would later become active in political life. In general, it was educated Catholic women professionals who were drawn to cultural nationalism, and it gave women the chance to contribute to Ireland's cultural life and justify their future political participation in the years before female suffrage.

Rapid social and economic changes had raised expectations among all sections of the bourgeoisie, but the path to higher status, particularly in public employment, was often blocked by Protestants. In time, therefore, cultural nationalism developed a strong populist Catholic edge. This sat uneasily with the Anglo-Irish literary revival, which was led by an elitist group of southern Protestants. Drawing on Irish folklore as the inspiration for their work, these artists were seeking to come to terms with their Irishness while occupying a marginal position on the fringe of the cultural nationalist development. Though a tiny minority, writers such as Yeats, Synge and Lady Gregory exuded such self-confidence and such a sense of intellectual superiority that they regarded themselves as the natural leaders of the emerging cultural movement. These activists had also been moved by the Parnell split, and by the circumstances surrounding the Chief's downfall, and this only added to their rejection of political nationalism. Clearly then, cultural nationalism emerged in the 1890s for a complex series of reasons, and this partly explains the tensions that surfaced within the movement in the early years of the twentieth century.

Of course, cultural nationalism did not begin with the Gaelic revival of the late nineteenth century. Indeed, many of the leading figures in the revival drew inspiration from the activities of the Young Irelanders who had sought to blend culture and politics in the 1840s. There were obvious parallels, because many of the Young Ireland writers were anxious to combat the increased anglicisation in Irish life in pre-famine Ireland. This intellectual backlash was led by Thomas Davis, who focused on Ireland's separate culture, language and race in highlighting the differences between Britain and Ireland. Of course, Davis was not the first Protestant to take an interest in Ireland's cultural heritage. Such interest had been particularly evident among elements of the Ascendancy class in the late eighteenth century, but Davis attached a clear political dimension to his cultural nationalism. Like many of his Young Ireland colleagues, Davis was uncomfortable with what he regarded as the narrow sectarian nationalism advocated by O'Connell. Clearly influenced by contemporary European developments, Davis articulated a romantic view of nationalism that emphasised the unity of all Irishmen, irrespective of their religion or class. His aim was to build a common sense of nationality among all Irishmen, which would be clearly rooted in the past. History, culture, music and the Irish language could all be utilised to raise national consciousness, and Davis intended to lead national opinion.

But Davis could not turn back the clock, and his thinking glossed over the very real religious and political difficulties which the more practical O'Connell fully appreciated. Though he denied it, Davis's view of Irish nationality was an elitist one, but this can be partially explained by his religion. With O'Connell making effective use of Catholic numbers, the only way for Protestants such as Davis to retain positions of leadership in Irish political life was through cultural nationalism. To educate the public on Ireland's distinctive culture Davis used the *Nation*. First published in October 1842, the weekly newspaper had an initial print-run of 12,000 copies, though it claimed a readership of 250,000 through its dissemination in the repeal reading rooms. The paper's original mission was 'to create and to foster public opinion in Ireland', but it really targeted the middle class in its efforts to teach nationality. Many of the *Nation's* reports mirrored stories in the contemporary British press. The paper's contributors and its audience tended to be middle class, English-speaking professionals from the towns. The newspaper cost a prohibitive 6d, and its distribution was mainly confined to Dublin, Leinster and south Ulster, the more urbanised, English-speaking and prosperous parts of Ireland.

Davis's death in September 1845, the subsequent Young Ireland drift into revolutionary nationalism, and the impact of the famine combined to sweep cultural nationalism off the political map. Yet Davis had left a deep imprint. While his call for the unity of Irishmen went unheeded, his belief that Ireland's distinct culture was the basis of Irish nationality provided the prop for cultural nationalists at the turn of the century. Yet cultural nationalism did not disappear entirely in the post-famine period. The Phoenix Society, founded in Skibbereen in 1856 by a local grocer, Jeremiah O'Donovan Rossa, was the best-known of a number of literary societies operating in County Cork. Attracting the shopkeepers, clerks and artisans from the ranks of the petty bourgeoisie, these clubs provided a forum for the discussion of advanced nationalist ideas, though they were soon to be swallowed up by the Fenian movement. Yet there was also a definite overlap from the Young Ireland days, and the Phoenix Societies kept alive the new approach to nationalism offered by Davis. There was considerable interest in the language and in Gaelic culture, as these small groups of men sought to rationalise their opposition to English rule. Later, a small group of literary Fenians, most notably Charles J Kickham, produced a series of patriotic ballads and novels, which enjoyed a wide readership among later generations of nationalists. Kickham's work looked back to a purer, simplified past, which elevated the landless labourer to hero status and firmly rejected the drift to commercialisation in rural Ireland. In his most popular novel, *Knocknagow*, which was published in 1879, Kickham depicted an idealised image of Irish society rather than reality. Yet this vision of Irish national identity exerted a very powerful influence on later nationalist leaders. Kickham painted a picture of a sensitive, conservative people, who had great pride in their local area and felt a real sense of belonging on the land. Above all, it was their religious faith, frugal lifestyle and anti-materialism that emphasised the Irishness of the peasantry.

Further evidence that there was an upsurge of nostalgia in rural Ireland and support for a new approach, which developed a separate expression of identity, came on 1 November 1884, when the Gaelic Athletic Association (GAA) was launched. Its founder, Michael Cusack, a teacher and sports enthusiast, had become convinced that the spread of English games such as rugby and cricket was having a detrimental effect on national morale. Previously, Cusack, who had taught at St Colman's, Newry, from 1871–74, had been a keen participant in both athletics and rugby, but his increasing interest in Irish culture saw him join the Society for the Preservation of the Irish Language in 1882. The primary aim of the GAA was to promote Irish sports and, from the outset, the movement enjoyed the full backing of Dr TW Croke, the Archbishop of Cashel, who was an outspoken critic of English cultural advances in Ireland. Together with his colleague, Maurice Davin, who had become the first president of the GAA, Cusack hoped that the movement would help to promote a stronger sense of Irishness. Indeed, Cusack and Davin never simply viewed the GAA as a straightforward sporting body but assumed that it would become part of a broader cultural reawakening. The movement was also a reaction against the middle class nature of pursuits such as rugby and cricket. Gaelic games were intended to be more plebeian in character, and there was a move away from the concept of the 'gentlemen amateur', who played such a prominent role in these more elitist sports.

Whereas Croke was an enthusiastic and committed supporter of the GAA, many clerics were initially hesitant about endorsing a movement which, it was feared, could become a rival to the church in rural Ireland. Very soon, however, the clergy recognised the popularity of a movement which provided new opportunities for organised recreational activity. Within two years of its formation it had 50,000 members, and the competitive element, which saw matches arranged between local parishes, ensured that the GAA contributed to the development of local patriotism. Most of these early members were farmers or farmers' sons, and they were joined by a small number of farm labourers. Although the GAA was essentially a rural movement, it also attracted clerks, shop assistants and other members of the commercial classes in the towns. In general, most of the early players were unmarried and Catholic. In the first All-Ireland hurling final to be played in Dublin in 1889, both county teams were drawn from single clubs. The winning Dublin team were nearly all drapers, who worked in stores such as Clery's, though most of them had originally come from Cork. At the national level the organisation of inter-county competitions saw the GAA play its part in the rapid growth of organised spectator sport, which was such a feature of the social history of the British Isles before the First World

War. The railway system was integral to this development, as special trains were laid on to take spectators to important matches. Extensive coverage of these games in the press also helped to generate a mass following for gaelic games.

Although it was essentially a cultural and sporting body, the GAA attracted its share of political interest. From the outset the movement secured considerable Fenian support. Adopting the policy of infiltrating suitable open nationalist organisations, the Fenian movement dominated the GAA's ruling executive within three years of its formation. Indeed, before the end of 1886, Cusack had been pushed aside, and Davin was the only non-IRB member still on the GAA executive. The Fenian initiative drew renewed hostility from sections of the Catholic Church, and this increased dramatically when the GAA threw its support behind Parnell during the split of 1890–91. This resulted in a sharp decline in GAA membership, as the church turned its fire on the movement in the years immediately following Parnell's death. Soon, however, the movement was reorganised and, now with the church's support, it began reversing the steep fall in membership, though Fenian infiltration continued. It was noticeable, however, that the GAA's recovery in Ulster ran well behind the other provinces. Still, on its formation, the GAA also won the backing of many prominent figures within constitutional nationalism, and it clearly benefited from the national self-confidence which Parnellism had bestowed on rural Ireland. Moreover, in its promotion of traditional Irish sports and its opposition to English games, the GAA could not avoid political controversy, and this gave militants within the movement repeated opportunities to articulate anti-English sentiment. In this way the GAA made an early contribution to the revival of national feeling in rural Ireland.

While the GAA found an eager audience in the Irish countryside for its blend of cultural and sporting activities, a literary renaissance was taking place in much grander surroundings. In 1885 Charles Oldham and TW Rolleston, both graduates of Trinity College, established the *Dublin University Review*, which provided a platform for those aspiring to a higher form of culture. The most notable figure in this Anglo-Irish literary revival was William Butler Yeats who established the Irish Literary Society of London in December 1891 and followed this with the launch of the National Literary Society in Dublin in May 1892. Writing in English, but drawing their inspiration from ancient Celtic myths and legends, Yeats and his followers sought to promote a more subtle sense of Irish identity that would stress an inclusive culture. For this, Davis provided the inspiration. In his work Yeats focused on themes that highlighted Ireland's separate cultural identity and, though Davis had stressed the importance of the Irish language, his mind was open to the notion that this new sense of Irishness could also be expressed in the English language. After Davis, Yeats looked for inspiration to two other celebrated figures, Standish O'Grady and Samuel Ferguson. Though Protestants like Davis, O'Grady and Ferguson were opposed to political nationalism, their keen sense of Irishness, combined with their outstanding literary talent, built a strong base for the next generation of cultural nationalists. Moreover, the non-sectarian nature of their work, which first popularised Celtic mythology, appealed to Yeats. These men were proud to be Irishmen but were also proud of their Protestantism, and they were committed to the belief that Ireland needed Protestant leadership. Yeats, of course, was from a landed gentry family in Sligo and he, too, was anxious that members of his caste would continue to assume positions of influence in a future nationalist, democratic Ireland.

It was the success of Parnellism in the 1880s that first encouraged Yeats and his fellow Anglo-Irish patriots to engage in the literary movement. Later, the death of Parnell and the subsequent petty squabbling of his former parliamentary colleagues were taken by Yeats and his followers as a signal to press the cultural alternative more aggressively. The role played by the Catholic Church during the split had increased the pressure on these patriotic intellectuals to develop their notion of inclusivity within the literary revival. Yet this was a forlorn hope. The literary revival struggled to break out of its tiny elitist circle and appeal to the mass of Irishmen. Yeats's associates – JM Synge, Lady Gregory, George Russell (AE), Edward Martyn and George Moore – took their inspiration from the ordinary people, but they were reluctant to come off their intellectual pedestals. They saw themselves as the artists of the national movement, engaged in the production of a new literature for an evolving country, and, though they recognised that they were a tiny minority, they played a crucial role in raising awareness of a distinct Irish culture.

It was another of Yeats's colleagues in the National Literary Society who succeeded in giving cultural nationalism a broader appeal. Douglas Hyde was the son of a Church of Ireland clergyman and he played a pivotal role in the Gaelic revival. Before going to Trinity College, Hyde had grown up in Frenchpark, County Roscommon, where he learned about Ireland's rich Gaelic heritage from local people speaking in their native language. Hyde wished to spark a revival of the Irish language, but he was also closely linked to Yeats and his circle of Anglo-Irish intellectuals. It was Hyde's inaugural lecture as President of the National Literary Society, delivered in November 1892, which provided the inspiration for the language revival in the 1890s. 'The Necessity for De-anglicising the Irish People' demanded immediate action to halt the decline of the language and then denounced the imitation of English manners and customs. Hyde's comments confirmed his nostalgic view of the past, and he was highly critical of the press and railways, the key agents of modernisation which, of course, had played such a crucial role in the development of political nationalism in the latter part of the nineteenth century. The lecture also set out Hyde's vision of a cultural revival which would be non-sectarian and non-political. This would, of course, encourage his fellow Protestants to play a full role in the language movement and, in articulating this notion of a cultural revival which would be above politics, Hyde was echoing the views expressed by Yeats. It was probably Hyde's influence that encouraged a significant number of Protestants to become early enthusiasts for the language revival.

Hyde's lecture had reawakened interest in the language movement and had encouraged a young Dublin clerk, Eoin MacNeill, to establish a new organisation. Previously, both the Society for the Preservation of the Irish Language, formed in 1876, and the Gaelic Union, formed in 1880, had campaigned for the greater use of the Irish language, but while they enjoyed a degree of success, their appeal was extremely narrow. MacNeill's new movement, the Gaelic League, which was established in July 1893, sought to revive Irish as a spoken and literary language. MacNeill had come from an Ulster Catholic middle class background and, like Hyde, had not been a native Irish speaker but had learned the language in an attempt to discover his own cultural roots. While working in Dublin, MacNeill had also carried out meticulous research into Ireland's Gaelic past. Indeed, his academic achievements saw him appointed to the first chair of Early and Medieval Irish History at University College Dublin in 1909. The third key figure in the formation of the Gaelic League was Father Eugene O'Growney, the Professor of Irish at Maynooth. These three pioneers of the language revival, a southern Catholic, a northern Catholic and a southern Protestant, stood at the head of the Gaelic League, and their varied religious and geographical backgrounds appeared to confirm Hyde's vision that the language would provide "a mental field upon which all Irishmen might meet". Although MacNeill shared many of Hyde's ideas, he was less willing to acknowledge the contributions of the mainly Protestant writers to the cause of Irish nationality, preferring to identify its roots in the remote Gaelic past. Moreover, in his desire to establish the Gaelic League as a truly popular movement, the more practical MacNeill assumed that this would require close collaboration with sympathetic elements of the Catholic clergy who had come under O'Growney's influence during their training at Maynooth. While his subsequent actions during the Easter Rising and his pro-Treaty stance have seen MacNeill cast as a moderate, such an assessment could not have been made in 1900. He was in full agreement with Hyde on the central importance of the language, which he viewed as the chief thread of nationality, but MacNeill was more insistent on the need for political autonomy. Moreover, in spite of the suspicions of a number of advanced nationalists, the Gaelic League, from its early existence, was linked with separatism.

The Gaelic League was to become the most important of the various movements engaged in cultural nationalism. Its nurturing of a national identity based exclusively on Gaelic culture and its emphasis on the revival of the Irish language distinguished the League from its more elitist predecessors. But the task of arresting the decline of the language was an extremely difficult one. The use of Irish had been in decline since the middle of the eighteenth century and, by 1801, only 50 per cent of the people spoke monolingual Irish. Its decline in the nineteenth century was spectacular. The impact of the famine greatly accelerated the trend, as the areas which suffered most were those same areas in the poorer parts of the west where Irish was most commonly spoken. By 1851 only 5 per cent of the population spoke monolingual Irish and over the next 50 years this figure dropped to 0.5 per cent. Even the number of bilingual speakers, those who spoke both Irish and English, was down to 14 per cent by the end of the nineteenth century. These figures emphasised the enormity of the task facing the Gaelic League. Indeed, its initial impact was disappointing. By 1897 only 43 branches had been established, as the League found it difficult to translate MacNeill's desire for a popular movement into reality. Certainly, Hyde proved his brilliance as a propagandist, and the League raised its profile by successfully campaigning for letters and parcels addressed in Irish to be accepted by the Post Office, and for bilingual street names and signposts to be accepted by Dublin Corporation. Yet these changes were merely cosmetic. If the language was to enjoy a sustained revival, the League would have to campaign successfully for Irish to become a compulsory subject in the school curriculum.

In addition to its attempts to revive Irish as a spoken language, the League ran language classes and Irish speaking social gatherings. Initially, only a section of the educated middle class was attracted by the League's programme in this formative period. While this included a small but significant number of Protestant enthusiasts, the majority of the early activists were respectable suburbanites who could be described as members of the Catholic intelligentsia. Although they regarded themselves as above politics, their rejection of English economic and cultural influences carried unmistakable political undertones. Even MacNeill, who consistently argued that the Irish nation had its roots in Ireland's ancient past and was not the creation of modern leaders such as Grattan, Tone or O'Connell, found it difficult to separate the pursuit of nationality from politics. Yet, while their membership numbers were not impressive, the energy and ability of the leadership laid secure foundations for future growth. By the end of the century interest in the League had increased sharply and, by 1901, the number of branches had risen to 100. It continued to expand in the early years of the twentieth century and, by 1904, the League had 600 branches with a total membership of approximately 50,000.

This rapid rise in membership was also attributable to two other factors which were to stimulate all forms of nationalism at the close of the century. Firstly, the centenary celebrations of the 1798 rebellion had stirred nationalist passions and benefited constitutional, cultural and revolutionary nationalism. Then, more significantly, the outbreak of the Boer War in October 1899 raised national feeling in Ireland, as all shades of nationalist opinion identified with the Boers in their struggle for independence against the might of the British Empire. The South African war had been a crucial factor in the reunification of the IPP, and many Irish MPs, notably John Dillon, took a passionate interest in the conflict. The war in South Africa had raised Irish national consciousness to a new level, and the consequent upsurge in anti-imperialist and anti-English feeling also aroused interest in cultural nationalism.

Therefore, while the death of Parnell and the subsequent schism within constitutional nationalism clearly boosted the cultural revival, and the Gaelic League in particular, its advance at the end of the nineteenth century was not due to further problems for the IPP. In fact, domestic and international events had combined to improve the prospects for all shades of nationalism, and reaction to the Boer War had stimulated cultural nationalism and political nationalism in equal measure. The numbers in the Gaelic League were now swollen by an influx from the ranks of the petty bourgeoisie, as clerks, shop assistants, civil servants and schoolmasters became interested in their cultural past. Another attraction was recreation. The first national festival was organised in 1897, and such events, while offering a focus and inspiration for the cultural revival in Ireland, also provided a social diversion for enthusiastic new members. One of the most important regional festivals was the Glens of Antrim Feis, which was first held in 1904. Promoted by Francis Joseph Bigger, a Belfast Protestant lawyer, who immersed himself in the cultural revival movement, the feis aimed to preserve the Irish language, traditions, songs, music and games for future generations. While the Irish dancing competition attracted great interest, the feis also promoted local industries, particularly traditional crafts such as weaving and basket-making.

The League organised a variety of social gatherings and pastimes which allowed its petty bourgeois members to engage with their own class and exclude all undesirables. Schoolmasters, in particular, played a prominent role in the growth of the League. While they frequently assumed the role of community leader, many of them felt insecure, underpaid and, consequently, discontented. For such people the League provided an outlet for their frustration and ambition. In addition, it offered an escape from some of the social pressures of modernisation that had become a key aspect of life at the turn of the century, particularly for elements in the petty bourgeoisie. Clearly, schoolmasters were very influential, and many pupils later recalled how their teachers indoctrinated them into radical nationalism. Moreover, teachers normally made the local schoolhouse available for evening language classes, which they themselves frequently conducted. In this they collaborated closely with the local clergy, as the priest often acted as the clerical manager of the local national school. This increased clerical participation further encouraged the growth of the League. By the turn of the century an increasing number of clergy had come to regard the Gaelic League as the best buffer against English popular culture, which was threatening to secularise Irish society and undermine the hegemony of the Catholic Church. In rural areas farmers' sons joined the local Gaelic League branch, but the movement was essentially an urban one. The irony was that the League never aroused anything like the same interest in the more remote Irish-speaking areas of the west.

A significant proportion of the new Gaelic League recruits were former emigrants who had recently returned to Ireland. Less inhibited by deference, the broader experience gained by such people had increased their self-confidence and made them more willing to challenge the status quo. For them, the Gaelic League proved a more attractive and exciting prospect than the outwardly conservative IPP with its ageing parliamentary representatives. Indeed, the majority of League activists were young, educated white-collar workers, many of whom were employed by the state, challenging an older middle class which was frustrating their political and social ambitions. Furthermore, this younger element demonstrated intellectual ambition, much of which was probably pretentious but nevertheless significant, and the League offered the opportunity for self-improvement and the realisation of this intellectual ambition. At the same time, these urban intellectuals were often scornful of the trappings of capitalist society, and they became fascinated by a romantic vision of an idealised Gaelic past, which was more egalitarian, viewing the simple life of the poor man as virtuous and fulfilling. Although similar political movements, which were romantic and visionary, were attracting the petty bourgeoisie in a new era of increasing democracy across Europe, the attack on materialism in Ireland became indistinguishable from an attack on Englishness itself. At the popular level, moreover, the Gaelic League increasingly defined Irish nationality in a negative manner by rejecting English influences and values.

If its growth around the turn of the century caused the League to become more political, it also made it more Catholic. This, in turn, made it less attractive to Protestants and a number, who had been active since the movement's formation, left the League. Through its official newspaper *An Claidheamh Soluis* (The Sword of Light), which was launched on 17 March 1899, the League engaged in a highly publicised series of clashes with the leading Trinity academic, John P Mahaffy, who wanted Irish taken off the intermediate school syllabus. Mahaffy was also critical of the Catholic clergy's interference at lower levels, and the League's rebuttal of his arguments raised public awareness of its work. In this regard, MacNeill, who was the first editor of *An Claidheamh Soluis*, was particularly effective in leading the opposition to Mahaffy. It was true, however, that in spite of Hyde's efforts to keep the League on an exclusively cultural footing, the early campaign against Mahaffy had given it a sharper political voice. The League attracted further attention when it campaigned successfully to have St Patrick's Day recognised as a national holiday. More significantly, the League won the right in 1909 to have Irish accepted as a compulsory subject for matriculation in the new National University. Hyde had led the campaign for compulsory Irish, and this threw the League into conflict with the IPP and John Dillon, who led the fight against compulsion. The mass membership, which such campaigns had helped to attract, was clearly more Catholic and more concerned with populist values.

The link between the Gaelic revival and Catholicism was most clearly articulated by DP Moran. A gifted journalist, Moran spent ten years working in London where he joined the city's Gaelic League branch. Returning to Ireland in 1898, Moran pronounced his shock at the damage done to Ireland by the rapid dissemination of British mass culture. In 1900 he founded the *Leader*, which first appeared in September and quickly became an instant success. Moran conveyed his personal disgust at the level to which Irish society had sunk, and he blamed this spread of English culture for the spate of gambling, drunkenness and immoral literature now destroying Ireland. Moran wanted to foster the language revival, but he warned against a preoccupation with Ireland's Gaelic past, arguing the case for a modern, competitive society on Irish terms. Through the advertising columns of the *Leader*, Moran urged his readers to reject goods that had been manufactured in England in favour of Irish-produced goods. His journalism also ridiculed the snobbery of the Catholic bourgeoisie, particularly in Dublin, which he regarded as an attempt to ape the manners of the English middle classes. While Moran had himself been educated at Castleknock College, a famous Dublin school that was visited by Queen Victoria during the royal tour of 1900, he was critical of the influence of English public schools on Ireland's leading educational institutions. In declaring his vision of an 'Irish-Ireland', a phrase that he coined, Moran viciously attacked the IPP, which he accused of negligence in its failure to protect Irish society against English cultural encroachments.

In addition to his sustained assault on constitutional nationalism,

Moran frequently attacked the separatist tradition and castigated Fenianism as an irrelevance. Not surprisingly, Moran's Irish-Ireland philosophy also led him into conflict with the Anglo-Irish literary clique. In his writing Moran dismissed the work of Yeats and his circle as a fraud, arguing that while it may have been Anglo-Irish, it was not Irish. While he shared Yeats's passion for nationalism, Moran utterly rejected Yeats's brand of high culture as irrelevant to the needs of Catholic Ireland at the beginning of the twentieth century. Along with Lady Gregory, George Moore and Edward Martyn, Yeats had founded the Irish Literary Theatre (subsequently the Abbey) in 1898. Their aim was to provide an opportunity for the creative figures in the literary renaissance to develop the Celtic theme in their work and take it to a wider audience. In this venture they were hounded at every turn by Moran who mocked the 'sham patriotism' of their work, describing it as 'un-Irish'. Relations between the Irish-Ireland and Anglo-Irish camps hit an all-time low in 1907 with the production of Synge's play, *The Playboy of the Western World*, at the Abbey. The play, in which a youth who kills his domineering father and then becomes the centre of attention for the local young maidens, reflected the generational tension in contemporary Irish society, but the *Leader* denounced it as 'pagan'. On its first night outraged Irish-Irelanders shouted down the actors, and the 'Abbey riots' continued for a full week.

But Moran's articles also carried a crude sectarian message. Nationalism and Catholicism were, for him, inseparable. Therefore, in spite of all his efforts, Yeats could not, in Moran's view, be truly Irish. He and his literary colleagues were denounced as 'West Britons', and the literary renaissance element of the Gaelic revival was effectively marginalised. Labelling Protestants as 'sourfaces', Moran accused them of discrimination against Catholics in employment and of diluting Irish nationalism in politics. Arguing that 'the Irish nation is de facto a Catholic nation', Moran rejected the nationalist claims of the Ascendancy class, as he urged Catholics to make use of their numbers and assert their supremacy. For Moran, this involved cultural and economic domination, as both were deemed necessary to create the conditions in which the new Catholic elite could force Britain to accept political autonomy for Ireland. This notion of a narrow, negative, but self-sufficient and fully independent, nationalism ran counter to the inclusive nationalism envisaged by Hyde. While Moran praised the Gaelic League for providing an Irish-Ireland alternative to English culture, he insisted that it, by itself, would never create the modern Irish nation that he desired. Moran's answer was to target the growing Catholic urban middle class and link their interest in cultural revival to achievable economic goals. Through their leadership Ireland would be transformed into a modern, self-sufficient, urban society, in which Irishmen would have developed the capacity to think and act as Irishmen. Privately, Hyde agreed with much of Moran's argument, though he recoiled from the populist tone of many of his articles. Moreover, the personalised nature of Moran's attacks often aroused controversy but, as an astute businessman with an eye on the *Leader's* circulation figures, this was unsurprising. In truth, Moran was simply articulating the logic of an Irish-Ireland view of nationalism. Gaelic culture was, for Moran, the culture of the Irish Catholic, and the Irish nation was a Catholic nation. Those Protestants who wished to identify with the Irish nation had to recognise this. For Moran, therefore, it was the struggle between Protestant and Catholic in Ireland that was of primary importance, rather than the struggle between Ireland and Britain which had been promoted by the various shades of political nationalism. Though an admirer of the Gaelic League, Moran advocated cultural nationalism based on exclusively Catholic and Gaelic values, and his Irish-Ireland movement was more overtly nationalist than the League.

Still, in spite of its claims, the rapid growth of the Gaelic League around the turn of the century saw it acquire a clear political dimension, which Moran and the *Leader* helped to foster. The cultural revival in general, and the Gaelic League in particular, became more closely identified with Catholicism, and the clergy took a more prominent role. Of course, within the broader sweep of new nationalism there were other small pressure groups that were more political in character. The Gaelic revival had encouraged the participation of a small but active Irish feminist movement. A Belfast-based journal, *Shan Van Vocht* (The Poor Old Woman), had been established in 1896 by the Protestant Alice Milligan and her Catholic associate Anna Johnston, both of whom were prominent Gaelic Leaguers in Ulster. The journal produced a series of literary and historical articles but also promoted separatist political ideas. When *Shan Van Vocht* ceased publication in 1899, its two founders cooperated with Arthur Griffith, another able journalist, who founded a new newspaper, the *United Irishman*. Griffith was a supporter of both the GAA and the Gaelic League, but his primary interest was in politics, where he hoped that the

IPP would give way to a more radical, separatist party. Drawing on political and economic ideas popular in contemporary Europe, Griffith established Sinn Fein (Ourselves) in 1905 to act as a rallying point for a variety of tiny radical nationalist groups, many of which had been spawned by the Boer War. One of the groups it incorporated was Inghinidhe na hEireann (The Daughters of Ireland), a more overtly political feminist organisation founded by Maud Gonne in 1900. In all of these organisations there was a considerable overlap of membership, with the Gaelic League retaining its dominant position.

The impact made by the League and the cluster of organisations labouring under the cultural nationalist umbrella must not obscure the fact that, in terms of numbers, cultural nationalism was very much a minority movement. The UIL had more members than the Gaelic League, and while the IPP never recaptured the energy and dynamism of the early 1880s, it remained an efficient political force enjoying the support of the vast majority of Irish nationalists. Indeed, the return of a Liberal government in 1906 gave a further boost to the IPP just at the point when the rise of cultural nationalism appeared to have peaked. Even the embryonic Irish labour movement stood comparison with cultural nationalism, as the Irish Trades Union Congress represented 60,000 workers by 1900. Of course, the role played by former Gaelic League activists in the 1916 Easter Rising conferred a retrospective significance on the movement. It is true that individual IRB members, particularly in Munster, joined the League soon after its formation, but the IRB only gained control of the movement in 1915. By that stage the League had become explicitly nationalist under the influence of these separatist infiltrators, and Hyde had resigned in protest. From the outset Hyde had wanted the League to stay aloof from politics, and he was adamant that it would not be attached to any political party. In this way it developed as a romantic and visionary movement that was anti-parliamentary in character. Yet, in spite of Hyde's protestations, it was clear that a movement inspired by nationalism would have to be political. In Irish society, moreover, where nationalism was such a pervasive influence, the Gaelic League was unlikely to escape its political clutches. It was left to Moran to administer a weekly dose of realism in the *Leader*.

In analysing the nature of cultural nationalism a number of historians have recently emphasised that the cultural revival was concerned with the invention of tradition, rather than the defence of a strong existing culture.

Hence, it can be argued that both the GAA and the Gaelic League were movements engaged in the creation of a separate Irish culture, rather than attempts to rekindle a lost past. Moreover, a comparison with the Welsh experience throws interesting light on the relationship between culture and politics. At the end of the nineteenth century cultural nationalism was a prominent feature of Welsh society and the use of the native language was much more widespread than in Ireland. In spite of the clear presence of a strong Welsh identity, there was no consequent rise in Welsh political nationalism. The Welsh were proud of their language and culture, but they were happy to remain part of the United Kingdom. In Ireland, by contrast, political separatism developed out of cultural nationalism.

# Chapter 6
# Defenders of the Union

U NIONISM AS AN ORGANISED political movement dates from 1885–86, when the crisis over Home Rule forced the defenders of the constitutional status quo in Ireland to come together to reject the nationalist demand for self-government. In large part, therefore, the Unionist movement that emerged in the late nineteenth century was a reaction to the challenge of Parnellism, though there was nothing natural or inevitable about the formation of this pan-Protestant alliance. The mass movement, which quickly developed and took advantage of the recent extension to the franchise, in the same way as nationalism, was an amalgam of social classes and diverse groups whose interests were often antagonistic. However, a unionist mentality predated this development. The introduction of the Act of Union had not created a pro-Union political movement. Instead, political support for the maintenance of the Union was part of the hidden ideology of both the Conservative and Liberal parties in Ireland, neither of which, of course, required a separate Irish leader. Consequently, there was a flow of ideas between Britain and Ireland, particularly on themes such as progress and reform, but also on fundamental principles such as the protection of property rights. Early unionism was instinctive and, from the outset, it was associated with the defence of the Protestant interest in Ireland. Significantly, Dublin, not Belfast, was the first city in Ireland to witness organised Protestant support for the Union, as Dublin Protestants combined to resist what they regarded as the erosion of Protestant privilege, which was being increasingly threatened by O'Connell's confident nationalism. Yet it is not sufficient to regard the emergence of unionism as just a negative response to assertive nationalism. There were positive reasons for maintaining the connection with Britain, as most Protestants assumed that the Union offered the best framework for continued social and economic progress. It was in Ulster, of course, that such a belief was most clearly articulated.

By the end of the nineteenth century Catholic nationalism had asserted itself as the dominant political force in Ireland. In the wider United Kingdom context the IPP had become the third party in British politics, and its influence at Westminster could not be discounted. It had been transformed by the electoral changes of the 1880s and by the emergence of a confident, middle class leadership. Mirroring this development, as the century progressed, the defence of the Union became increasingly, but not exclusively, associated with the Irish Protestant interest. Yet this was a reversal of the pattern at the time the Union was enacted. Its most implacable opponents in 1799–1800 had been those members of the Protestant Ascendancy who refused to waver in the face of either financial inducements or political pressure from Westminster. At the time these men rejected Lord Clare's central argument that only the Union could provide an effective defence for the Irish Protestant nation. However, this sentiment did not last. While the Anglo-Irish opponents of the Union were proud of the Irish nation and proud of their Irishness, they soon realised that it was pointless to continue the struggle and they quickly reconciled themselves to the Union, knowing that there was no prospect of reversing the decision. Indeed, little changed in the years after the Union. The Irish Parliament had gone, but Protestant fears over concessions to Catholics did not materialise. The Ascendancy class, in general, began to appreciate Pitt's argument that they would be more secure as a majority in the United Kingdom than they would as a minority in Ireland. The price of this security, of course, was the surrender of power to Westminster.

Catholics, on the other hand, had mixed views on the Union. While O'Connell and the small group of Catholic lawyers had opposed the Union from the start, other Catholic elements, notably the church, had given the measure some degree of support, convinced that the new constitutional arrangement was preferable to the Irish Parliament. This optimism, however, quickly dissipated. Having failed to overcome opposition from both English and Irish Protestants, Westminster could not meet Catholic aspirations. Consequently, Catholic resentment grew and this culminated in a sustained demand for the return of an Irish parliament in Dublin, as Catholics increasingly blamed the Union for all of their social, economic and political grievances. In this way religion became a key component of Irish nationalism. With Protestants uniting to defend the Union, political division in nineteenth-century Ireland was characterised by a clear sectarian division. While there was, of course, some deviation in both religious camps, it was never sufficient to alter the pattern which was established in Irish politics during the nineteenth century. The failure of successive Westminster governments to grant emancipation in the early years of the nineteenth century drove a wedge between Catholics and the British state and, simultaneously, intensified the sectarian divisions in contemporary Irish society.

The greatest influence on the development of Protestant politics in the first half of the nineteenth century was Daniel O'Connell. Under his leadership Catholics united and organised efficiently to make use of their numerical superiority. In the 1820s and 1830s O'Connell effectively broke the landlords' control over their tenants at elections, as he mobilised the Catholic population in the successful campaign for Catholic emancipation. His fiercest critics had been the Irish Tories, who had consistently opposed Catholic concessions since the 1790s. In the years immediately after the Union, these same Tories had thwarted Pitt's attempts to carry emancipation. However, the formation of the Catholic Association in 1823 presented a new challenge for Irish Toryism. In rousing the Catholic political nation, O'Connell inadvertently contributed to the development of a new Protestant political consciousness. Moreover, Irish Tories learned the art of party organisation directly from O'Connell. An Irish Protestant Conservative Society was formed in 1831, shortly before a general election and in preparation for the changes envisaged in the Great Reform Act of 1832. This body monitored the work of local registration clubs whose concern was to maximise the Tory vote in all elections. Again following O'Connell's example, these clubs were often controlled by members of the Protestant clergy who regularly resorted to unscrupulous methods in their eagerness to register Tory supporters. Still, in spite of a restricted franchise that favoured property at the expense of Catholic numbers, the O'Connellites won 39 seats to the 30 seats won by the Tories in the general election of 1832. Clearly, Irish Toryism needed a broader appeal as O'Connell turned his fire on the Union itself. In 1836 the Irish Protestant Conservative Society gave way to the Irish Metropolitan Conservative Society, a more moderate body reflecting the changes that Peel had introduced to English Conservatism in his attempt to modernise the party and capture the popular vote. In the following year's general election more efficient organisation and extra funds led to Tory victories in 34 seats, and this figure climbed to 40 in the 1841 general election.

Such was the Conservative party's efficiency at elections that the Tories continued as a powerful force even after the extension of the franchise in 1850. The number of voters in Ireland more than trebled to 164,000, and this encouraged the formation of an Independent Opposition party which went on to form a distinct group at Westminster. The new party won 48 seats in the 1852 general election, though this figure included a significant number of MPs who declared themselves in favour of an independent party after the election in addition to those who had committed themselves to the Independent Opposition cause in their election addresses. However, the new movement, which had appeared as a major threat to Liberal and Conservative dominance, lacked effective leadership and was soon torn apart by internal disagreements. Consequently, the traditional political forces quickly regained control, and the Conservative party won 54 seats, its highest total since 1829, at the 1859 general election, leaving it, for a brief period, as the largest party in Ireland. Out of a possible 66 contests for the 105 seats – all of the county seats and 6 of the boroughs returned 2 MPs, with Dublin University also electing 2 MPs – there were 27 contested seats, for which the Tories had a campaign fund of £7,800. This great financial advantage, together with the work done by Conservative registration societies, helped the party to maximise its electoral support. While many Catholics had voted for Conservative candidates in 1859, the party's strongest support came from members of the Church of Ireland. Conservatives were elected in every province, but the party won more than half of its seats in Ulster. Here, the party had active societies in towns such as Cavan, Banbridge and Ballymena, and most of these bodies were run by Church of Ireland clergymen. These activists worked on the assumption that only the Union could protect the Protestant interest. At this point, while the Liberal MPs were both Protestant and Catholic, Conservative MPs were exclusively Protestant.

Earlier, in demonstrating their electoral ability, the Irish Tories had frustrated the anticipated domination of the O'Connellite party. Indeed, in the euphoria of the emancipation triumph, O'Connell himself had confidently predicted the collapse of Irish Toryism, or the 'Orange party', a term which he used frequently to describe his electoral opponents. The Orange Order was a Protestant political society, which spread quickly from its south Ulster base at the end of the eighteenth century. With a reputation for extremism and aggression, the Order was initially boycotted by most of the landowning class, but O'Connell's success in the 1820s and the growing threat of Catholic power brought a change in outlook. In spite of its volatile nature, Irish Tories recognised the Order's political potential, and the relationship between Toryism and Orangeism improved significantly in the late 1820s, as increasing numbers of the gentry class joined the Order. By this stage its membership approached 100,000. The Orange Order was a direct consequence of the rising sectarian disorder in south Ulster, particularly in County Armagh, where clashes between the rival factions increased sharply in the 1790s. Of course, sectarian bitterness had a long history in this area, but, towards the end of the eighteenth century, fierce economic competition between the two religious groups added a new dimension to the problem. Armagh was the most densely populated county in Ireland and competition for land was fierce, as farmer-weavers on both sides of the religious divide fought for their share of the lucrative linen trade. The result was a series of violent clashes, culminating in a mini-battle at the Diamond near Loughgall in September 1795. Following their victory the Protestants marched to Loughgall, where they formally established the Orange Order. Soon, the Order was associated with the bloody suppression of the 1798 rebellion and was drawn into politics by the impending Act of Union. After some initial hesitation most elements in the Orange Order opposed the Union. It regarded the Irish Parliament as the best defence of Irish Protestant interests, and it feared that the Union would ultimately result in the concession of Catholic emancipation.

However, the success of O'Connellism transformed Orange thinking on the Union. Activists within the movement were drawn towards Irish Toryism and the Order played a prominent role in its support for Conservative candidates during election periods. Although it had become increasingly involved in mainstream politics, the Order could not shed its violent image. Frequently, its actions created unwelcome publicity and, in spite of its pleas of loyalty to the British Crown, successive Westminster governments regarded it as a threat to public order and sought to weaken its influence. In 1825 it was temporarily suppressed, along with the Catholic Association, but was soon revived. Then, in 1836, following a highly critical parliamentary report, which uncovered evidence of deliberate Orange infiltration in both the yeomanry and the army, the Order was formally dissolved. Thereafter, it survived in semi-underground fashion and continued to exercise influence at local level, where it occasionally orchestrated violent sectarian clashes. By the mid-1840s the movement had been revived, and it quickly renewed its links with Irish Toryism. By this stage its reputation had again reduced the numbers of participating gentry, but it was significant that it had acquired a substantial Presbyterian membership in the north. This was important, because the vast majority of the Order's early members were Church of Ireland, but, by the 1830s, the Episcopalians and Presbyterians in Ulster had tentatively moved closer together. A key advocate of closer cooperation between the Protestant denominations was Reverend Henry Cooke, a Presbyterian cleric from County Down. Cooke had been engaged in a fierce theological struggle with the liberal wing of Presbyterianism, which was led by Reverend Henry Montgomery.

By the late 1820s Cooke's conservative faction was in the ascendant and, following his victory over Montgomery, he became publicly associated with Irish Toryism. In October 1834, in an address to an O'Connell-style monster meeting, he told 40,000 Protestants gathered at Hillsborough, County Down, that they must work together to combat the growing Catholic threat. Although his theological campaign had rallied a majority of Presbyterians against the liberal wing of the church, Cooke failed to lead a large body of his co-religionists to question their political support for the Liberal party in Ulster.

While Cooke never persuaded a majority of Presbyterians to ally with Irish Conservatism, he did succeed in exploiting Protestant fears of Catholicism and probably contributed to the formation of a Protestant political consciousness. Still, he did not steer Ulster Presbyterians away from radical politics. They had become disillusioned in the immediate aftermath of the 1798 rebellion, and, while many had been sympathetic to emancipation in principle, they particularly distrusted O'Connell and the rest of his Catholic agenda. Cooke articulated these fears and he spoke for the vast majority of Presbyterians in his opposition to O'Connell's repeal movement. He frequently led the response to O'Connell's anti-Protestant rhetoric and organised the opposition to O'Connell's Belfast visit in 1841. At the subsequent Conservative celebrations, Cooke's speech highlighted the economic success of Belfast, arguing that future prosperity depended on the Union. Indeed, a *Northern Whig* petition to Queen Victoria in October 1843 urged special treatment for Ulster in the event of repeal. The *Whig*, the leading organ of the liberal press in Ulster, highlighted the differences between the Saxon and Celtic races, claimed by the advocates of repeal, and called for Ulster's inhabitants to be given the right to continue to live as 'fellow subjects' with their fellow citizens in the British Isles. Although most Presbyterians continued to support the Liberal party in the mid-nineteenth century, Cooke's efforts had made Irish Toryism, hitherto anathema, more respectable in Ulster Presbyterian eyes. In promoting the Irish Conservative cause, Cooke also maintained close links with English Conservatism, and his influence helped to draw Irish and English Conservatism closer together. For Cooke this was a natural process and it countered the alliance between O'Connellite nationalism and the Whig party in Britain. In this way Cooke helped to lay the foundation for the future link between Irish unionism and the British Conservative party.

The increasing prosperity of Belfast, to which Cooke had alluded in 1841, strengthened the case for the defence of the Union. The city grew even more quickly in the second half of the nineteenth century, as the introduction of engineering and shipbuilding added to the established textile industry. Booming industrial expansion attracted thousands of prospective workers eager to improve their economic lot and escape from the endless cycle of rural poverty. In the middle of the nineteenth century this urban migration was disproportionately Catholic. In 1800, an estimated 10 per cent of Belfast's 20,000 population was Catholic, but, by the census of 1861, 34 per cent of Belfast's 121,000 population was Catholic. The increasing prosperity of Belfast in the mid-nineteenth century coincided with the fatal collapse of the Irish rural economy and, as Catholics occupied the least secure position in rural Ulster, the famine surely increased the trend of Catholic urban migration. For their protection each religious community tended to live in segregated areas, and it soon became possible to identify both Catholic and Protestant working class districts of the city. The influx of new workers raised sectarian tension in the city to new levels, and minor incidents occasionally led to serious rioting between the two communities. In 1857, 1864 and 1872, rioting erupted in July with the approach of the 'Twelfth' celebrations and continued for much of the summer, causing serious loss of life and widespread damage.

Key religious and political events in the 1850s and 1860s helped to shape Ulster Protestant politics. Cooke continued to warn of the Catholic threat to Protestant liberties, and the American-imported, great evangelical revival of 1859 brought together Protestants of all denominations, creating a new spiritual consensus and emphasising the differences, political as well as doctrinal, between Protestants and Catholics. At the same time, the Orange Order increased its influence in Belfast's Protestant working class districts. One of its principal leaders from the early 1860s until the end of the century was William Johnston, a small landowner from Ballykilbeg, County Down. In February 1868, Johnston was given a one-month jail sentence for his role in leading an Orange march in defiance of the Party Processions Act, which was used by the authorities to ban all Orange and other potentially explosive marches between 1850 and 1872. Treated as a martyr by the Belfast Protestant working class, Johnston stood as an independent in Belfast in the general election of November 1868 and trounced his Conservative opponent. Although his victory dismayed the Conservative squires leading the party, they recognised his electoral appeal in the wake of the 1867 Reform Act, which enfranchised skilled workers. After his success as an independent he was endorsed as a Conservative party candidate and, following a redistribution, he held the South Belfast seat until his death in 1902. Johnston's rise to prominence was significant because it marked the beginning of a powerful link between Orange populism and the Conservative party in Ulster.

The leaders of Belfast's thriving business community were predominantly middle class Presbyterians and, as their primary concern was the establishment of trading links with Britain for their export-oriented businesses, they had little attachment to the rest of Ireland. Indeed, this wealthy bourgeoisie naturally shared the concerns and aspirations of the urban, middle class elite on the mainland. Belfast was, in many ways and for a variety of reasons, much more like Liverpool, Manchester or Glasgow than it was like Dublin. From the early part of the nineteenth century there is evidence of a growing attachment to Britain, which went some way towards eradicating the influence of those radical Presbyterians who had turned against British rule in the 1790s. For such people, France, not Britain, quickly became associated with tyrannical rule, and Presbyterians were prominent in the celebration of famous British victories over the French such as Trafalgar. In time, many of these radicals found common ground with reformist elements in Britain. Yet these developments did not automatically translate into support for the Union. For this a combination of the reaction to O'Connellism, particularly the campaign for repeal which drew a sharp response from Ulster, and the spectacular economic growth of Belfast from the 1820s was necessary. While the Irish Tory party had responded negatively to the O'Connellite threat, the emergence of a self-confident, largely Presbyterian bourgeoisie in Belfast led to closer integration with Britain.

O'Connell's principal opponent when the repeal issue was debated at Westminster in 1834 was James Emerson Tennent, the Conservative MP for Belfast. Tennent, who was first elected in 1832, represented a new form of Irish Conservatism, which was closely linked to Peel's brand of progressive conservatism on the mainland. Unlike traditional Irish Toryism or Orange loyalism, this new creed, propagated by Tennent, endorsed a series of progressive policies, including parliamentary reform. While the traditional Tories concentrated on defending the status quo and looked back for inspiration and reassurance to Protestant heroes such as Oliver Cromwell and William III, industrialists in Belfast looked forward to further progress, improvement, reform and prosperity by maintaining and developing the link with Britain. Not surprisingly, this drew these progressive Conservative elements into closer cooperation with local Liberals, a factor that subsequently facilitated the formation of the pan-Protestant alliance which underpinned political unionism. Of course, local loyalty was a powerful factor in all parts of Ireland, but the Presbyterian bourgeoisie offered a distinct contrast to Ulster's landlords, who were usually members of the Church of Ireland and shared a much greater sense of community with their fellow church members in the three southern provinces.

In the second half of the nineteenth century the number of Protestants in Leinster, Munster and Connacht was close to 250,000, or 10 per cent of the total population. This figure included the landed gentry and a large group of urban professionals, particularly in Dublin and Cork, but it also included many shopkeepers, farmers and labourers. For the most part, these southern Protestants were well scattered and it was only in a few isolated areas that they were able to mount a serious electoral challenge with the prospect of victory. Their electoral capacity had been seriously damaged by emancipation and by the various alterations both to the franchise and to the constituency boundaries that had occurred in the middle of the century.

Still, they were well organised, and bodies such as the Central Conservative Society, formed in 1853, were able to seize the few electoral opportunities that presented themselves. Not surprisingly, it was the families of the landed interest who played the dominant role in Conservative politics in the three southern provinces.

Yet it would be wrong to assume that this landed class was exclusively Protestant. In the late eighteenth century Catholics owned approximately 5 per cent of the land in Ireland, but by the 1870s this figure had almost trebled. The Catholic gentry included some of Ireland's major landowners, including the Earl of Kenmare who owned more than 118,000 acres. Catholics had taken advantage of the Encumbered Estates Courts, which had been established under the Encumbered Estates Act of 1849, to buy property from insolvent Protestants. There was also a significant minority of Catholic landlords who had converted from the Protestant faith. These included Lord Granard, the Earl of Dunraven and William Monsell who was MP for County Limerick from 1847 to 1874. These Catholic landlords were usually Liberals, as they opposed the Tory party's continued support for the Church of Ireland up to 1869. While they had been strong supporters of Catholic emancipation, they were firm opponents of repeal, and later Home Rule, which they felt would ultimately destroy the social system in Ireland. Like their fellow Protestant landlords, these Catholic supporters of the Union often exhibited a dual nationality. They regarded themselves as Irish and British. Many of them came from families that had lived in Ireland for hundreds of years, and they were resident landlords who were committed to Ireland. From this number there were many, such as Monsell, who had been educated in England, and the bonds with the mainland were further strengthened by growing inter-marriage between families on both sides of the Irish Sea. Of all the supporters of the Union, it was this privileged landed elite that felt most threatened by the advance of Irish nationalism in the last quarter of the nineteenth century.

The key factor in the subsequent organisation of political unionism, the movement to defend the Union, was the alliance of the Ulster bourgeoisie and the Irish landlords, a reversal of their historic antagonism. This alliance was, of course, born out of political necessity, and tension was never far from the surface. On the positive side, however, the alliance enjoyed great social standing, with easy access to British high politics, and real financial muscle. This partly explains its extraordinary resilience in the face of the great Home Rule struggles at the end of the nineteenth and beginning of the twentieth centuries.

For Protestants living in southern Ireland the Church of Ireland played a crucial role in providing a focus for scattered, sometimes vulnerable, communities. Indeed, the boost given to the Church of Ireland by the impact of the evangelical revival had increased the sense of purpose and influence of the established church. Later, in tandem with Irish Toryism, the Church of Ireland mounted a determined, but ultimately unsuccessful, struggle to stop Gladstone's disestablishment plan. Catholic nationalism had long demanded disestablishment, and the 1869 Irish Church Act formed a major plank in Gladstone's new Irish strategy. It also coincided, as Gladstone recognised, with a major triumph for Irish Liberals in the general election of 1868, when they won 66 seats. Gladstone was quick to take advantage of what appeared to be a solid Catholic/Presbyterian alliance on the issue of disestablishment. Such a rapprochement was, of course, tactical and temporary, and, in the end, disestablishment removed a major bone of contention between the Church of Ireland and its Presbyterian counterpart. Therefore, disestablishment in 1869 paved the way to greater Protestant unity, which, in turn, eased the task of transforming unionism from a political slogan into an organised political movement.

In the 1868 general election a clear pattern was discernible. Members of the Church of Ireland voted Conservative, while Catholics and most northern Presbyterians voted Liberal. At the time, therefore, Irish politics appeared to be an extension of British politics, as the two great parties, Liberal and Conservative, competed for power. The advent of Butt's Home Rule organisation, and its initial success at the 1874 general election, broke this pattern. Constitutional nationalism consolidated its position in the 1880 general election, as Home Rulers were returned in 62 seats, leaving the Conservatives with 26 and the Liberals with 15 seats. Therefore, unionism did not respond immediately to the challenge of Parnellism. At this point the earliest and most energetic element in the pro-Union cause was the landlord class in all parts of Ireland. Landlords saw the agrarian agitation as a direct threat to their dominant position in Irish society. In addition to this class dimension, landlords also viewed the agitation in sectarian terms. This was particularly true in the north, where the landed interest enlisted the enthusiastic support of the Orange Order, which, of course, already had close links with the Conservative party, in countering the land agitation.

Although the Land League initially enjoyed considerable support among the north's tenant farmers, it soon came to be regarded as a nationalist front, and the Orange Order was able to provide a cross-class Protestant alliance to repel the agrarian threat in Ulster. Very soon, the Order was providing a solid organisational base for the development of political unionism, and its ability to paper over class and denominational cracks within Protestantism made it a vital element in the creation of a viable political alternative to nationalism. However, the downside to the Order's involvement was that it limited unionism's appeal outside the Protestant population and, in so doing, reinforced the sectarian nature of Irish politics.

Of course, a crucial factor in the development of both unionism and nationalism was the 1884 Representation of the People Act, which increased the Irish electorate from 224,000 to 738,000. In enfranchising farm labourers and small tenant farmers the legislation boosted constitutional nationalism, which now threatened to take Conservative and Liberal seats in Ulster, where Protestant numbers were concentrated. Indeed, awareness of the growing nationalist threat in the province had already been heightened by Tim Healy's by-election success in North Monaghan in June 1883. Subsequently, nationalists loudly proclaimed that 'the invasion of Ulster' had begun. Again, it was the Orange Order that was first to respond to this nationalist advance, organising a series of counter-demonstrations, including the infamous incident at Rosslea, County Fermanagh, in October 1883, when a large number of troops had to be deployed in order to prevent serious disorder. When a nationalist rally had been planned for the village, the Order quickly called a counter-demonstration, bringing in some 7,000 supporters from neighbouring counties. Shots were fired as the Orangemen, led by Lord Rossmore, refused to have their march re-routed. As tension rose throughout the province, these incidents became more frequent and, naturally, politics became even more polarised.

The obvious determination of nationalists to increase their representation in Ulster and the changes made to the franchise qualification in 1884 demonstrated the urgent need for Protestant unity. Healy's by-election victory had raised the number of Home Rule MPs in Ulster to three, but it was clear that nationalists would increase this figure substantially at the next general election. The experience of the previous quarter of a century had indicated that the Conservatives, rather than the Liberals, offered the most effective opposition to the growth of nationalism. It was the Conservative party, therefore, that provided the major influence in the early development of unionism. The Conservatives had already established close links with a reinvigorated Orange Order, and the Order played a crucial role in the general political mobilisation of the 1880s. At the same time, unionism benefited from the emergence of much greater Protestant solidarity and from a general feeling of superiority, which had been evident for most of the century. This gave early unionists an unshakeable confidence in spite of their numerical disadvantage. The key to the success of unionism would be the remarkable coalition between landed and business interests, both of which regarded the defence of the Union as essential to their future prosperity.

*Chapter 7*
# The Organisation of Unionism

T HE FORMATION OF EXPLICITLY Unionist organisations began in 1885. With a general election expected and Parnellism threatening to sweep all before it, the Irish Loyal and Patriotic Union (ILPU) was founded on 1 May 1885. The initiative had been taken by a small group of southern landowners and academics, whose aim was to coordinate electoral opposition to Home Rule candidates. Among those who were most anxious about the threat of Home Rule and the prospect of Catholic domination were a group of academics from Trinity College, Dublin, traditionally the seat of learning for the Protestant Ascendancy. These men led the initial drive against Parnellism. The group included the Provost of the university, Reverend JH Jellett and two future Provosts, Anthony Traill and JP Mahaffy. Equally concerned by the prospect of Home Rule was a larger body of southern landowners, and a number of these, such as Viscount de Vesci and Lord Castletown, helped to promote the ILPU. Unionism in its earliest organised format, therefore, was a party of education and property. These landowners had been rocked by the agrarian chaos directed by the Land League and by the consequent increase in class tension, and the ILPU, therefore can be partially viewed as a reaction to the land agitation of the 1880s. Moreover, the launch of the ILPU coincided with the formation of a number of groups dedicated to the protection of landlords and their tenants who faced mounting problems in 1885, as instances of boycotting by Parnell's National League multiplied in certain areas. One of the most important of these landed bodies was the Cork Defence Union, formed on 28 September 1885 at a meeting of landlords organised by AH Smith-Barry, later Lord Barrymore, who was to become a leading figure in Irish unionism. Not surprisingly, there was considerable overlap in membership between bodies such as the Cork Defence Union and the ILPU.

In the general election of November–December 1885 the ILPU sought collaboration between Conservatives and Liberals in the southern provinces, and offered support to any candidate who pledged himself to defend the Union. The recent dramatic increase in the franchise accounted for the unexpected optimism among ILPU activists in the run-up to the election. Nevertheless, an indication of the vulnerability felt by pro-Union supporters in the south was the delay in the public announcement of the formation of the ILPU until October 1885, one month before the general election. Indeed, though it was very active in the election, distributing large numbers of pamphlets, the existence of such a hostile political climate meant that much of its work had to be done discreetly. The ILPU supported 52 candidates in the general election, but there were no successes. In fact, the only two pro-Union victories in the south were the two unopposed candidates for Trinity College. While ILPU-backed candidates had won a respectable share of the vote in some Dublin constituencies, other results must have been acutely embarrassing for the fledgling organisation. For example, the anti-Home Rule candidate in Kerry East, Charles Henry de Grey Robertson, polled only 30 votes, which represented less than 1 per cent of the total votes cast in the constituency. The failure of the ILPU to make any electoral impact was disappointing, but its supporters were not disillusioned and their determination to thwart the Home Rule designs of their lower class political and religious opponents remained strong. Its predominantly landed leadership had been alarmed by the activities of the Land League in the early 1880s, and they feared that a Home Rule parliament, dominated by their enemies, would either force them out directly by confiscating their lands, or indirectly through penal taxation. WEH Lecky, the famous historian who held one of the two Dublin University seats from 1895 until his resignation in 1903, expressed this view most emphatically. Lecky recoiled from the notion of Catholic democratic rule, stating that this fellow Irish Unionists might just have accepted a Home Rule parliament dominated by the Catholic gentry, but they could not stomach the thought of a parliament in Dublin controlled by their former class enemies in the Land League, who were "supported by the votes of the peasantry ... and subsidised from America by avowed enemies of the British empire". Meanwhile, in the ILPU's first pamphlet, the fear of higher taxes was cited as the most important reason for rejecting Home Rule.

After their initial electoral foray the ILPU reassessed its strategy. While the 1885 general election had highlighted the futility of contesting seats in the south, the movement's leaders appreciated that some form of constituency organisation should be developed in order to maintain morale among pro-Union supporters. Two other options remained open and both were tried. The ILPU had many contacts in British politics, and its members could use their influence on the mainland to encourage their parliamentary friends at Westminster to stand firm in the face of nationalist pressure for Home Rule. Another ploy was to develop close cooperation with their allies in Ulster, where there were obvious electoral possibilities. In the northern province, meanwhile, considerable consternation was caused by the announcement of Gladstone's conversion to Home Rule following the general election. The election itself had a sobering effect on the Conservative party in Ulster. It won 16 seats to the 17 won by nationalists. The Liberals were left without any representation, but their participation had undoubtedly cost the Conservatives a number of seats. Gladstone's sudden move and the normal post-election analysis of results had forced opponents of Home Rule to come to terms with their differences. Initially, opponents of Home Rule in Ulster had looked towards the ILPU to coordinate Unionist opposition across all four provinces, but some Ulster Protestants were soon expressing the view that there were special issues at stake in the north of Ireland. The lead was taken by a number of Conservative landowners who founded the Ulster Loyalist Anti-Repeal Union (ULARU) on 8 January 1886. From the outset the ULARU was active in staging a series of meetings across the province, and it moved quickly to establish close relations with both the Orange Order and the Protestant Churches.

The new movement received a boost from the highly publicised visit of Lord Randolph Churchill to Belfast in February 1886. The ULARU had undertaken much of the organisation for the visit, and Churchill delighted an Ulster Hall audience of Conservatives and Orangemen when he assured them that the Conservative party in Britain would back them in their hour of need. Churchill's sentiments are important, as they marked a symbolic commitment by the Conservative leadership to their Irish cousins in the struggle against Home Rule. Yet in playing 'the Orange card' Churchill was clearly guilty of political opportunism, as his real aim was to exploit Gladstone's conversion to Home Rule, and the consequent opposition in Ulster, to advance the Conservative cause in Britain.

Indeed, the announcement of Gladstone's support for Home Rule in December 1885, and the subsequent formation of a Liberal government on 30 January 1886, made the introduction of a Home Rule Bill inevitable. It was with this prospect in view that a number of Ulster MPs with Orange connections had come together on 25 January to create a separate Irish Unionist party in Parliament. The inspiration for this move had come from Colonel Edward Saunderson, a County Cavan landlord and leading figure in the Church of Ireland who had represented the county as a Liberal MP from 1865 to 1874. The Land War, however, had altered Saunderson's political views, and he joined the Orange Order in 1882 before being returned as the Conservative MP for North Armagh in 1885. In turning to the Orange institution Saunderson was seeking some form of defence against the growing threat of the Land League, and he was quickly joined by a number of other Protestant landlords who viewed the Order as a potential vehicle for landlord resistance to agrarian radicalism. Two Fermanagh landlords, EM Archdale and JH Crichton, later the fourth Earl of Erne, and their County Monaghan neighbour, Lord Rossmore, became very prominent in the early 1880s, and their action conferred a new respectability on a movement which had suffered from a chequered reputation in the past. Significantly, the attraction of the Orange Order made more impact in these south Ulster 'border' counties where the combined challenge of the Land League and Home Rule party was most keenly felt by the landowning class. Consequently, this group of south Ulster gentry enjoyed a disproportionate influence on both the Orange Order and the emerging Unionist movement. Saunderson was the first leader of Irish unionism and he directed the party's attack on the 1886 Home Rule Bill.

Yet Saunderson was a complex character. His Liberal party background saw him eager to promote a non-sectarian unionism, but his passionate commitment to the Orange Order and the recognition of the Order's crucial organisational role for unionism ensured that his wish would never be realised. Ideologically, he believed in a form of Tory paternalism that was based on a landlord-led Protestant alliance. In spite of his obvious Conservative sympathies, Saunderson was convinced that Irish unionism should have its own distinct voice at Westminster. Only by developing this self-reliance and freedom of action, he argued, could the long-term security of loyal Irishmen be protected. In fact, Saunderson had been urging the formation of an independent party at Westminster since the previous year, warning of the Conservative party's lack of concern for loyalists in Ireland. This sense of urgency increased when, in the second half of 1885, it appeared that the Conservatives might opt for an alliance with Parnellism. By introducing his Home Rule Bill, Gladstone had simplified the situation for Saunderson, but he continued to campaign for a strong, independent Irish Unionist voice at Westminster and remained wary of his Conservative allies.

If Gladstone had clarified the position for Saunderson, he had thrown Ulster Liberalism into confusion. On 19 March 1886 a Liberal convention of 600 delegates met in Belfast to discuss recent events and inform Gladstone of their views, but no consensus was reached. However, the introduction of the Home Rule Bill on 8 April finally forced Ulster Liberals to face reality, and the majority decided to join with their old Conservative foes and oppose Home Rule. This was confirmed on 13 April when the Liberal deserters joined Conservatives in a great Ulster Hall protest meeting. Still, this was a bitter pill for many of these former Liberals to swallow and, though they had to acknowledge the weight of Conservative numbers, they struggled hard to retain a distinct identity within the broad Unionist movement. Led by Saunderson, the Irish Unionist MPs uttered vague warnings about the outbreak of civil war in Ulster in the event of Home Rule being enacted. In Ulster, meanwhile, rumours were circulating that the Orange Order would raise a paramilitary force to resist Home Rule, and there was wild talk of thousands of men receiving military training. Nationalists never took such threats seriously. They dismissed rumours of armed resistance as fantasy but, though their assessment in the summer of 1886 was probably correct, nationalists made the initial, and fatal, error of underestimating their opponents' determination to resist Home Rule. Following the Home Rule Bill's defeat in June 1886, Gladstone sought to win popular support for his new policy in a general election. In the seven months since the previous election Ulster politics had been transformed. A parliamentary Unionist party had emerged under Saunderson's leadership, and Gladstone's Home Rule gamble had destroyed, with one stroke, the Liberal party in Ireland. In Ulster the Unionists won 17 of the 33 seats, though two of the victorious Unionists were described as Liberal Unionists. The general election of July 1886 had demonstrated that the Union was by far the most important issue in Ulster politics. A clear unionist/nationalist rivalry had been established as Ulster society was increasingly polarised on religious grounds. In fact, the election had been held against a background of serious violence in Belfast. The Home Rule crisis had obviously raised the sectarian temperature and trouble flared in June following a row at the shipyard. The violence continued until September, claiming around 50 lives and ravaging working-class districts in the city.

The Liberal defeat in the 1886 general election and the return of a Conservative government under Lord Salisbury saw the Home Rule danger pass, if only temporarily. Thereafter, Saunderson was impressed by Arthur Balfour's tough security response to agrarian disorder in the south, but he was undoubtedly perturbed by the Conservative government's land legislation, fearing that some form of compulsory purchase might be introduced. This was a concern that he shared with his fellow landlords in the rest of Ireland. While he recognised that the electoral success of unionism depended primarily on Ulster Protestant support, Saunderson viewed the party which he led as an Irish party. Although he sat for North Armagh, his residence in County Cavan allowed Saunderson to empathise with southern gentry living in predominantly nationalist communities. Moreover, his landed and Church of Ireland background meant that he shared essential common interests with the landlord class in the south and west of Ireland. Indeed, it was the challenge faced by these Irish landlords which had a crucial impact in the early development of unionism. Yet the success of the land agitation, which had squeezed concessions from the British government, indicated that the landlord class was in steady decline. This made its alliance with the Ulster bourgeoisie vital to the success of unionism. While this new form of unionism was essentially the creation of the Home Rule crisis, it is wrong to view the movement simply in negative terms. In Parliament its leaders frequently expressed their political beliefs using negative and antagonistic language, particularly in this formative period, but there was more to unionism than the defence of Protestant privilege in Ireland. It had solid foundations, building on the organisation and structure of the Irish Conservative party, and it took advantage of the easing of denominational differences within Protestantism. Maintenance of the Union was seen as essential to future social and economic progress in Ireland. At the same time, unionism benefited from the emergence of a distinct British identity that was, in part, a response to the advance of Catholic nationalism and, more significantly, the result of Ulster's economic development.

The general election results of 1885 and 1886 had highlighted the boundary that existed between north and south. There was, moreover, a difference in emphasis in the cases that southern and northern Unionists presented in their rejection of Home Rule. The isolation and vulnerability felt by southern Unionists, who frequently withdrew to the sanctuary of the 'Big House', accounted for their more reasoned and less aggressive opposition to Home Rule. Southern Unionists were more tolerant of the Catholic religion, partly because their lack of numbers outside Dublin made them much more reliant on local Catholics whom they employed in a variety of occupations. Outside Ulster, Unionists also distanced themselves from most of the wilder, sectarian rhetoric and, not surprisingly, the safeguarding of civil and religious liberties never featured as prominently on the southern Unionist agenda. Many were, moreover, more liberal in their politics. Lecky had stated that he never considered religion in presenting the case against Home Rule. For him Home Rule was a question between individual freedom and organised tyranny, or, as he bluntly argued, between loyalty and treason. In fact, southern Unionists were not exclusively Protestant. A significant number of Catholic landowners, lawyers and ex-soldiers shared an instinctive conservatism with their southern Protestant neighbours. Such Catholics had done well out of the Union and they were not convinced by the nationalist argument in favour of Home Rule.

Perhaps the best known Catholic Unionist in the south was the lawyer William Kenny, who was the MP for the St Stephen's Green division in Dublin from the general election in 1892 until his appointment as a judge at the end of 1897. In this prosperous Dublin constituency Kenny enjoyed substantial Catholic middle class support in both his 1892 and 1895 election triumphs. While his 1892 victory was attributed to the nationalist split, as both Parnellite and anti-Parnellite candidates stood, Kenny enjoyed a decisive win against a single, prominent Home Rule opponent at the 1895 general election. In his opposition to Home Rule Kenny emphasised the commercial argument in favour of retaining the link with Britain and warned against a likely breakdown of law and order if the Union was broken. Both of these arguments struck a chord with a section of the Catholic middle class in Dublin. Moreover, in their pamphlet literature, southern Unionists consistently pointed out that the great majority of Catholic landowners were Unionist. One of the most prominent Catholic Unionist landowners was Lord Fingall who owned over 9,500 acres in County Meath.

In addressing a Unionist gathering in 1892 Fingall had actually argued that the most instinctive and national political stance for Catholics to adopt was one of support for the Union. Another very prominent Catholic Unionist in the early period was the distinguished Trinity academic, Dr Thomas Maguire, who was Professor of Moral Philosophy at the university. Maguire insisted that Home Rule would result in clerical interference in education, particularly higher education. In an 1886 article he had warned about placing education in the hands of the bishops, as the Catholic laity would never seek to be independent and could be expected to back the bishops on every issue. Maguire claimed that there was a Catholic bias against higher education, which would be revealed under Home Rule. Higher education, in Maguire's view, encouraged independent thought and prompted individuals to question religious truths, thus leading him to conclude that university teaching undermined clerical control.

All of these southern Unionists were much more concerned with the threat that Home Rule posed to Irish society and, more particularly, to their own privileged position. In spite of their lack of numbers, their social standing, which was clearly under fire in the last two decades of the century, instilled a confidence that allowed them to come to terms with their lack of electoral support. Some indication of their social and economic dominance in Irish society towards the end of the nineteenth century can be gleaned from a close look at the reception committee chosen for the great southern Unionist demonstration in Dublin in November 1887. In addition to the governor and the directors of the Bank of Ireland, the committee included 34 directors of public companies, 101 deputy lieutenants and JPs, 124 barristers, 65 physicians, 445 merchants and 28 fellows and professors from Trinity College. This constituted the cream of Irish society, its wealth, power and intellect, and it was this instinctive feeling of superiority among southern Unionists that lay behind their self-confidence in politics.

While their numbers in the House of Commons were limited, southern Unionists did enjoy considerable influence at Westminster, where they appeared to have direct access to the corridors of power. In 1886, 116 of the 144 peers with Irish interests had connections with southern unionism, while a small number held parliamentary seats in the south of England. Indeed, southern Unionists were much more closely integrated with British Conservatism than their Ulster colleagues, a situation which owed much to the existence of close family ties between the two groups. Furthermore, a significant number of these more prominent families owned estates in both Ireland and England. In this way southern Unionists shared many of the anxieties felt by British Conservatives when they looked at the likely impact of Home Rule, and they tended to have a broader, less parochial view than their Ulster colleagues. These concerns centred on the damage that the concession of a Home Rule parliament might inflict on the integrity of both the United Kingdom and the British Empire. An indication of the Conservative party's interest on the issue came with the decision taken in the summer of 1886 to alter the party's name to the Conservative and Unionist Party, and the labels 'Unionist' and 'Conservative' became interchangeable.

Still, it was evident that the Conservative party's concern for Ireland was more tactical than genuine. This was most clearly revealed by Churchill's reckless intervention in Ulster, but the temptation to exploit emerging Unionist reaction to Home Rule attracted other leading figures in the Conservative hierarchy. Opposition to Home Rule gave Conservatives the opportunity to attack their political opponents and to appeal to the British electorate. Irish Unionists, particularly those in the south, had also taken a keen interest in British voters. With the knowledge that any Home Rule Bill would have to secure a majority in the House of Commons, southern Unionists, who could make little electoral impact in Ireland, began to target marginal seats in Britain. Salisbury's convincing victory in 1886 had reinforced the idea that the key battleground for the maintenance of the Union was in Britain. From the outset, then, southern Unionists bombarded selected constituencies in Britain with anti-Home Rule propaganda, and they maintained a constant channel of communication with supporters on the mainland. Southern Unionist morale received a further boost with the Parnellite split of 1891. This led to the formation of the Irish Unionist Alliance (IUA), which superseded the ILPU.

Again, the landlord class was to the fore. Among Protestants in the south and west, the commercial and professional classes, while they were often sympathetic to the cause, were usually reluctant to become openly involved, fearing that their participation would have a detrimental effect on businesses which were heavily dependent on Catholic custom. The IUA adopted an ambitious programme, hoping to organise constituency branches in the south, with further plans for multiple sub-branches. Early encouragement came from its two successes in St Stephen's Green and South Dublin in the 1892 general election which, when added to the two

Trinity seats, gave the Unionists a total of 23 seats. Soon, however, the IUA was forced to recognise its limitations and, by 1906, it had abandoned its plans for constituency branches. Though the IUA failed to become a mass party organisation, it played a crucial role in directing the anti-Home Rule campaign in Britain through its London office. Moreover, in spite of their numerical constraints, southern Unionists often played the dominant role within unionism in these formative years. Well funded and efficiently organised, they were first to react to the dangers presented by Parnellism. At the outset it was the landlord class, stirred by Colonel Saunderson, who organised Unionist forces in Ulster. For these leaders, Ulster Protestants, with the Orange Order in the vanguard, offered the best protection against the rural chaos threatened by nationalist land agitators. Indeed, Irish Unionists were united by the fear that those directing the agitation might soon hold office in a Home Rule administration. There was also broad agreement among Unionists on the contention that Home Rule would never satisfy Irish nationalists. Saunderson and others frequently quoted nationalist leaders when they claimed that Home Rule would push open the door to complete separation. In 1886, however, Ulster Unionists tended to emphasise the religious objection above any other.

In addition to the obvious geographical difference, there was a distinct class difference between the two Unionist groups. This was clearly illustrated at the Ulster Unionist Convention in June 1892. In opposition Gladstone clung to his belief in Home Rule, and the trend of Liberal by-election successes raised the prospect of a new Liberal government. With a general election pending, leading Ulster Unionists were determined to organise a display of defiant opposition to Home Rule in an attempt to influence opinion in Britain. The Convention was a major propaganda success. A great wooden pavilion had been constructed to hold the 12,000 delegates from all over Ulster. The Duke of Abercorn chaired the proceedings, and the 400-strong platform party represented the cream of Ulster society, with prominent landowners and business leaders very much to the fore. Yet the delegates comprised a broad cross-section of Ulster society, with at least one-third being drawn from the tenant farming class. The initiative in organising the Convention had been taken by the ex-Liberal MP, Thomas Sinclair, who now chaired the Ulster Liberal Unionist Association. Sinclair was determined to refute the claim made by Gladstone's Liberal supporters and Irish nationalists that unionism represented the interests of only the small landed elite, desperately clinging to their exalted status in Ireland and guilty of stirring up sectarian feeling in order to defend their privileges.

Sinclair's purpose was, therefore, to impress on English opinion that unionism was a broad church, representing a wide variety of interests. It was, of course, this cross-class alliance within Ulster unionism which allowed it to develop as a dynamic political movement capable of mobilising Protestant opinion in the province. Ultimately, this set it apart from southern unionism. Perhaps, not surprisingly, many of the speakers at the Convention tended to emphasise Ulster resistance to Home Rule, even though there were frequent references to the all-Ireland nature of unionism. Interestingly, it was also evident that the majority of the speeches were moderate and measured in content, suggesting that the enactment of Home Rule would provoke a huge passive resistance campaign in the province, rather than anything approaching civil war. Although Ulster unionism had, from the outset, a distinct militant style, something which was particularly evident in the period before the First World War, the reality did not match the rhetoric.

In these early years, however, the focus of Unionist opposition to Home Rule was parliamentary. Gladstone had, as Unionists feared, triumphed in the general election of July 1892. By this stage of his career Ireland was his burning passion, and it was the unfinished business of pacifying Ireland that justified the ageing leader's decision to continue at the head of the Liberal party. Gladstone had responded to the demonstration of defiance at the Convention by arguing that Unionists, who rejected the democratic wishes of a majority of the Irish people, were being unreasonable. As the Liberals were dependent on the IPP to give them an overall majority, it was inevitable that a second Home Rule Bill would follow. When it was introduced in February 1893, there was a flurry of activity among Unionists. In Ulster an attempt was made to mobilise grass roots supporters, and a number of organisations sprang up in an attempt to take advantage of the heightened tension. In addition, the Conservative party again tapped into anti-Home Rule feeling in Ulster, and a succession of Tory luminaries, including Arthur Balfour, Joseph Chamberlain, the Duke of Devonshire and Lord Salisbury himself, crossed to the province in a repeat of Churchill's 1886 visit to remind Ulster Unionists that the Conservative party would not desert them in their hour of need. Significantly, these morale-boosting visits frequently included speaking engagements in Dublin, where large audiences of Unionist supporters could be guaranteed. In Parliament, meanwhile, the debates on the second Home Rule Bill generated fierce rivalry. These debates dragged on for more than 80 days, as Saunderson and his Unionist colleagues took a leaf out of Parnell's book and resorted to delaying tactics whenever possible. Saunderson was also at the centre of the famous Commons' incident on 27 July 1893, when proceedings had to be suspended following an unsightly brawl in the chamber. The fact that this shocked many Conservatives did not perturb the Unionist leader. In his long experience of challenging Parnell, Saunderson had clearly been influenced by Parnell's leadership style and tactics, and he showed little regard for the negative impact that Unionist excesses might have on Conservative support in Britain.

Unionists, particularly in Ulster, celebrated the outright rejection of the second Home Rule Bill by the House of Lords as an outstanding triumph. Gladstone retired in March 1894 and, with his successor, Lord Rosebery, determined to avoid further Home Rule controversy, Unionists could breathe easily. The subsequent Conservative victory in the general election of July 1895 reinforced this new sense of security. In the process of thwarting Gladstone's Home Rule ambitions, a number of important differences had emerged between supporters of the Union in Ulster, the rest of Ireland and Britain. Occasionally, these tensions would surface, but the Unionist alliance maintained a united front until the second decade of the twentieth century. By the time of the second Home Rule Bill Ulster Unionists had developed a powerful regional identity, though they were perfectly content to work within the broad Irish Unionist front. The role played by the landed leadership was crucial to this. More than other Unionists, the gentry class regarded themselves as Irish. Yet, from 1886 onwards, the bourgeoisie was gradually eroding the power of the landlords within unionism. In 1886 landlords held 50 per cent of the Unionist seats in the House of Commons, but this figure had fallen to 33 per cent by 1900, and would fall further. As the bourgeoisie, domiciled primarily in north-east Ulster, replaced the landed class, Ulster unionism became more self-reliant. Up to 1900, however, unionism functioned as a formidable movement because of the effective cooperation between Irish landowners and northern business leaders. These emerging middle class figures, many of whom had extensive industrial interests, were growing more anxious about the damage that Home Rule would inflict on the province's economic prospects. Indeed, there was considerable speculation that a number of Belfast's leading firms, including Harland and Wolff, would re-locate to Britain should Home Rule be enacted. In fact, the economic case against Home Rule was most clearly articulated by Sinclair. He warned that a Home Rule parliament would have devastating consequences for Ulster business, as firms would find it impossible to raise finance for investment on the capital markets. In fact, the economic case against Home Rule was most clearly articulated by Thomas Sinclair. He warned that the introduction of devolution would cause a crisis of confidence in the capital markets, which would prevent Ulster's substantial businesses from raising finance for investment purposes. While these economic concerns were undoubtedly genuine, it was the religious factor that proved most successful in mobilising Protestant opinion in the north. Thus, 'Home Rule means Rome rule' became the rallying cry of Ulster unionism.

Although the broader Unionist family tolerated this appeal to sectarian tribalism in times of crisis, it could cause acute embarrassment among Unionist supporters in Britain and the rest of Ireland. For Conservatives, the key issue was the threat that Home Rule posed to the Empire, a concern which was shared by southern Unionists.

In truth, outside the family connections, Conservatives cared little for Ireland. While they identified strongly with Ulster resistance to Home Rule in 1886 and 1893, it was apparent that much of their defiance was reserved for periods when they were out of office. Although the fight against Home Rule strengthened the bonds between British Conservatives and Irish Unionists, each group was careful to protect its independence. Irish Unionists were never subject to the rigid discipline that Parnell imposed on the IPP and, during long periods of Conservative rule, Unionist MPs sometimes acted in a disunited and haphazard fashion. Any threat to the Union, however, led to a rapid closing of ranks. Still, most Unionist MPs showed little interest in British affairs. As the great majority of these MPs were Ulster Unionists, the term 'Ulster party' was often used to describe this distinctive Westminster grouping. While they were viewed as the Conservative party's natural allies and though they enjoyed some influence with the Conservative party, particularly with Lord Salisbury, these 'Ulster party' MPs were consistently wary of placing too much trust on their Tory allies. In fact, one historian has described the Ulster Unionist relationship to the British state as 'contractarian'. Unionists had colonised Ulster in the seventeenth century on England's behalf and, if the British state now reneged on its part of the 'contract' by imposing Home Rule and betraying Unionists to their enemies, then they would be absolved from any obligation to obey Westminster's laws. Thus, unionism, or loyalism, was based on an external relationship to the British state, rather than any real feeling of belonging to the British nation.

While this argument may have some merit, it does not take sufficient account of the growing sense of Britishness felt by many Unionists at the end of the nineteenth century. Indeed, unionism had also borrowed heavily from the ideology of late nineteenth-century British imperialism, which focused on the civilising impact of British rule and fitted neatly with ideas of Anglo-Saxon Protestant superiority. This allowed Unionists to undermine the nationalist argument that Home Rule enjoyed overwhelming support in Ireland and cast some doubt on the suitability of the Catholic Irish for self-government.

Unionist unity, then, was conditioned by an assessment of the seriousness of the nationalist threat. When this subsided following the defeat of the second Home Rule Bill, class divisions within unionism quickly surfaced. At the heart of this upheaval was the long-running dispute between landlord and tenant, and this problem was particularly acute in Ulster. Although the effect of denominational differences within Protestantism had been reduced by religious developments in the second half of the nineteenth century and by the unifying influence of the Orange Order, it was still strong enough to cause disruption in the north. This meant that the sometimes difficult relationship between Church of Ireland landowners and their Presbyterian tenants could be further strained by perceptions surrounding these denominational loyalties. Unlike Catholics, who often viewed their landlords as foreign oppressors, Presbyterian tenants had allied with the northern gentry in galvanising Unionist opposition to Home Rule. These Ulster tenants now expected to reap the benefits of their political support. At the same time, however, the landed class, typified by the attitude of Saunderson, was determined to defend landlord rights. A potentially disastrous situation in Ulster's rural constituencies was only averted by the land reforms introduced by the Conservative government at Westminster. Ulster's Presbyterian tenant farmers found a champion in Thomas Wallace Russell who had become Liberal Unionist MP for South Tyrone in 1886.

Building on his core support among Presbyterian farmers in rural Ulster, Russell launched a popular campaign in the winter of 1894–95 aimed at pressurising the Conservative government to deliver land reform. Naturally, this drew him into conflict with Saunderson and the other landlord MPs who held out against reform. Much of what Russell advocated was included in the Conservatives' 1896 Land Bill, but, angered by what he regarded as the uncaring attitude shown by northern landlords to their Presbyterian tenants, he continued to press for radical changes. Yet Russell was distinguished by his ability as well as his radicalism. Both Arthur Balfour and Joseph Chamberlain held him in high regard, and he was regularly invited to Britain to speak on behalf of Conservative candidates engaged in by-elections. In 1895 he was appointed as a junior minister in the Local Government Board, but ministerial office failed to dilute his radicalism on the land question. When he began a new wave of land agitation in the late summer of 1900, he was dismissed from the government. Much to Saunderson's horror, Russell was now advocating compulsory land purchase, and this led to a serious rift between him and other Unionist MPs.

Although the leadership isolated him, Russell could not be ignored as his agitation for further land reform continued to attract tenant farmer support. By 1901 he had established his own organisation, with the intention of mounting an electoral campaign against Unionists. This move was successful, as Russellite candidates overturned Unionist majorities in the East Down and North Fermanagh by-elections in 1902–03. In both of these contests, victory was guaranteed by the action of Catholic tenant farmers who joined with their Presbyterian counterparts to defeat the Unionist candidates. Earlier, Saunderson, in spite of his impeccable Orange credentials, had found himself under serious pressure in holding off an independent opponent in his North Armagh seat in the general election of 1900. There was widespread disaffection among North Armagh's tenant farmers, and the Unionist leader was accused of neglecting his constituents during his 15 years as their representative. Yet the class politics that Russell had championed could not survive.

The shock of the 'devolution crisis' of 1904–05 once again raised the prospect of Home Rule, and Russell's electoral base was rapidly eroded as Unionists appealed for solidarity in the face of this perceived nationalist threat. It was the bourgeois element within Ulster unionism that led the fight back against Russellism. These middle class leaders had been alarmed by Saunderson's failure to repel the Russellite challenge, and they were convinced that unionism desperately needed to find some way of channelling popular opinion. Their actions led to the appearance of a more localised form of unionism, which sidelined Saunderson and his landowning colleagues. Indeed, Saunderson's position had been further undermined by a sustained attack from the populist Protestant leader Thomas Sloan, who won the South Belfast seat in a 1902 by-election and held it against the official Unionist challenger until 1910. Sloan, who enjoyed the support of loyalist ultras in Belfast, had savagely criticised Saunderson for being soft on Catholicism, and he led a breakaway faction to form the Independent Orange Order in 1903. One consequence of these political developments around the turn of the century was the formation of the Ulster Unionist Council (UUC) in 1905, a body that ensured much greater grass roots participation within unionism and guarded against the threat of internal division.

The establishment of the UUC had shifted the focus within unionism towards a more representative and localised movement. Unionism ceased to be a predominantly parliamentary movement as the bourgeois element in Ulster seized the initiative. While the possibility of a rift between northern and southern unionism was now more likely, this was averted until the pressure of the next Home Rule crisis in 1913. Still, the logic of a more cohesive, popular movement in the north, which the new leaders deemed essential for Unionist electoral survival, was the development of a more self-reliant movement, less concerned with the particular problems facing Unionists in the south. Up to 1900, however, landlord influence, though in decline, ensured that unionism was, for the most part, united. Southern Unionists had enjoyed a disproportionate influence and this helped to ensure regional harmony, while the emphasis on parliamentary activity allowed Unionists to develop close links with their British Conservative allies. Russell's agrarian campaign in rural Ulster had highlighted damaging social divisions within the movement, but the emerging bourgeois leadership in the north eventually responded and managed to restore solidarity. In overcoming the Russellite threat and re-establishing class consensus within northern unionism, these new middle class leaders had found a local solution to a local problem. Indeed, Saunderson and the old landed elite were increasingly irrelevant to the construction of a more dynamic populist movement, which encouraged greater grass roots participation and was more suited to the changing demands of people politics. If Saunderson and his landed colleagues were now considered peripheral figures, so too were southern Unionists. It was among southern Unionists that the decline of Irish landlordism was most keenly felt. The gentry class had been the driving force within southern unionism, particularly outside Dublin, but the steady erosion of landlord power towards the end of the nineteenth century weakened the movement, both politically and financially. The problems facing southern Unionists reinforced the determination of Ulster's new middle class leadership to take more responsibility for their own security.

There were, however, other problems undermining southern unionism. Southern Unionists were divided on the best strategy to maintain the Union. More enlightened elements favoured some kind of accommodation with moderate nationalists, but they faced a larger group of rejectionists who frowned on all attempts at reconciliation. The key figure among the moderates was Horace Plunkett, the MP for South Dublin. Plunkett was convinced that economic progress based on improvements in agriculture would overcome political division in Ireland. While he was firmly opposed to Home Rule, Plunkett advocated a progressive strategy aimed at reconciling the nationalist population to the Union. The key for Plunkett was wholesale improvements in agriculture which, he argued, would transform the Irish economy and lead to a reassessment of the Union. Before entering politics Plunkett had been a prime mover in the establishment and development of the Irish cooperative movement. Its aim was the modernisation of agricultural processing and marketing through the creation of a large number of mini-enterprises, which were funded by the pooling of local capital. Plunkett's vision was of a reconstructed rural economy and society which, ultimately, would radically alter attitudes to the national question. But Plunkett extended the principle of cooperation beyond the opening of new creameries. Following the general election of 1895, in which he retained his South Dublin seat, Plunkett called for representatives of both nationalism and unionism to meet for a discussion on the future economic development of Ireland. With a Conservative government in place at Westminster and Home Rule off the agenda, Plunkett assumed that the timing was right for his initiative. Although there was opposition from Unionist and nationalist leaders, a Recess Committee, so called because it met during the parliamentary recess of 1895–96, met to explore issues of common concern.

In 1896 the Recess Committee published a unanimous report, suggesting that consensus politics might replace the old divisions. The Recess Committee endorsed Plunkett's demand for the creation of a department of agriculture in Ireland and the provision of technical instruction. Certainly, the Conservative administration at Westminster was encouraged by the work of the Recess Committee. The new cross-party spirit of cooperation fitted neatly with the Conservative policy of 'constructive unionism', which ran from 1895 to 1905. This was the Conservative response to the Liberals' Irish strategy, and its aim was to achieve steady economic and political progress on a broad front, in a way that would undermine the nationalist demand for Home Rule and reconcile a majority of Irishmen to the Union. Gerald Balfour, the Chief Secretary for Ireland from 1895 to 1900, had coined the phrase, "killing Home Rule with kindness", and he shared Plunkett's view that a commitment to economic improvements, particularly in agriculture, could rob nationalism of much of its appeal. Recent scholarship has cast doubt on the existence of such a coherent philosophy within constructive unionism, suggesting that much of the legislation introduced by Balfour and his successor, George Wyndham, should instead be seen as a series of pragmatic responses to particular problems around the turn of the century. Nevertheless, there had been a long history of British statesmen, notably Peel and Gladstone, pursuing constructive policies with the intention of ameliorating Irish conditions and, in so doing, limiting the economic appeal of nationalism. Indeed, most leading nationalists were convinced that Balfour's programme represented a direct threat to Home Rule. Dillon refused to sit on the Recess Committee, and he warned fellow nationalists to avoid being sidetracked from the legislative goal of Home Rule by the allure of consensus politics. Only the Liberal alliance could, he argued, deliver Home Rule, and he was highly suspicious of Conservative or Unionist requests for cooperation.

Dillon's caution meant that he was slow to recognise the significance of Balfour's 1898 Local Government Act, which allowed the Irish party to gain control over most county, urban and district councils, particularly in the three southern provinces. In the following year, Balfour introduced the necessary legislation to implement the recommendations contained in the Recess Committee's report. Suitably impressed by Plunkett's detailed knowledge of agriculture, Balfour created a new Department of Agriculture and Technical Instruction, and installed Plunkett as the body's first vice president. Earlier, Balfour's 1896 Land Bill had provided additional funds for land purchase and removed some of the obstacles discouraging tenants from buying their farms under previous legislation. Of course, the high point of the Conservative administration's land purchase policy was the 1903 Wyndham Act. It transformed Irish society by turning huge numbers of tenants into owner-occupiers, but, contrary to Conservative hopes, it failed to check nationalist impetus. Plunkett's vision of new consensus-style politics and cross-party cooperation, set against a background of growing economic prosperity based on the modernisation of Irish agriculture, had proved too optimistic.

For his part, Saunderson was dismayed by the Conservatives' betrayal of Irish landlordism. He viewed the land legislation as concessions to agrarian agitators who would never be satisfied, and he consistently used his influence with Salisbury to curb the reformist tendencies of the Conservative administration. Naturally, Saunderson had also been angered by Plunkett's unorthodox brand of unionism, and he shared Dillon's suspicions of the Recess Committee and consensus politics. Although a landlord himself, Plunkett's constant criticism of his fellow landlords enraged the Unionist leader. In fact, Plunkett's attitude and his reformist zeal also infuriated many of his constituents, and he lost his South Dublin seat at the 1900 general election due to the intervention of an independent Unionist candidate. Plunkett's political demise had demonstrated that southern unionism was not powerful enough to accommodate both reformist and mainstream factions. Still, in these formative years from 1885 to 1900, southern Unionists exerted a major influence on the new political movement. Social confidence and political know-how meant that the endangered landed gentry were first to react to the Home Rule threat, while enthusiasm for the Unionist cause was evident among all sections of the Protestant community in Dublin. Consequently, unionism was essentially an Irish movement during these early years, and it was effective because of the easy relationship between Irish landlords and Ulster bourgeoisie. In time, however, these regional and class differences would become more pronounced, and it would become more difficult to hold this broad Unionist alliance together. The threat posed by Russell had undoubtedly added to this difficulty. In the end, it was Ulster's unique experience of industrialisation and, more particularly, northern Protestant control of this experience, which gave unionism a much more obvious Ulster focus in the early years of the twentieth century.

Although unionism is best understood as an all-Ireland movement in the period 1885–1900, its development at grass roots level reflected regional diversity. The ILPU, which was overtaken by the IUA in 1891, organised Unionist opposition to Home Rule in the south, while the ULARU took the lead in directing northern unionism. Subsequently, other Unionist movements sprang up in the north. The Ulster Convention League was formed in 1892 to oversee the arrangements for the great Unionist demonstration held in Belfast in June 1892. Two attempts to give northern unionism a broader base followed. The Unionist Clubs Council was established in 1893 to encourage the formation of Unionist clubs across the province. Similarly, the Ulster Defence Union was formed in March 1893 to make preparations for resistance to Home Rule. It was a more representative body with a central assembly of 600 elected by Unionist members. This assembly then chose 40 representatives who joined with Ulster Unionist peers and MPs to form an executive council under the chairmanship of Thomas Sinclair. The executive council of the Ulster Defence Union acted as the directing authority of Ulster unionism, and it was from this body that warnings of arming and drilling emanated. By 1895, however, these organisations had lapsed, as the threat of Home Rule abated with the return of a Conservative government. Before this, the Orange Order had played the key role in mobilising the Ulster Protestants in defence of the Union. The Protestant extremist, Lord Rossmore, had been one of the first to recognise its importance, when he stressed that only the unique characteristics of the Order could have facilitated an alliance between landlord and tenant. The other key organisation was the Church of Ireland. With its parishes spread across the entire island, the church helped to knit together isolated Protestant communities, and it gave unionism an obvious Irish dimension by the close of the nineteenth century. Landlords were, of course, prominent figures in both the Church of Ireland and in the emerging Unionist party, and their contacts with the Conservative party in Britain naturally enhanced Irish Unionist influence at Westminster. Significantly, many of these landlords, particularly in the south, had little difficulty with the concept of dual nationality, as they saw no contradiction between being both Irish and British.

*Chapter 8*
# Conclusion

D EVELOPMENTS IN BRITISH POLITICS early in the twentieth century appeared to have rescued nationalism from the self-inflicted damage of the Parnellite split. After its long period of domination, the Conservative party had quarrelled with itself on the issue of tariff reform, bringing the Liberals back to power. Initially, with such a commanding majority, there was little incentive for the Liberal government to take any further risks on Irish Home Rule. However, this situation changed in 1910, when two further general elections produced hung parliaments. The Liberals continued in government, but they relied on the IPP for an overall majority. With the IPP holding the balance of power, the prospects for Home Rule appeared bright, and Dillon's faith in the Liberal alliance was vindicated. Moreover, the eruption of a constitutional crisis had led to the 1911 Parliament Act, which removed the Lords' veto and cleared the main obstacle to Home Rule. A third Home Rule Bill duly followed in 1912 and, with Westminster politics now poisoned by the controversy surrounding the constitutional crisis, the Conservative party gave its full backing to Unionist plans for opposition.

Nevertheless, constitutional nationalism appeared to be within touching distance of success, and all threats of Unionist resistance were dismissed as fanciful. At this point the Unionists found a champion who would channel popular Unionist opposition. Edward Carson had clearly learned from Parnell, and the style of militant constitutionalism that he deployed was reminiscent of Parnellism in its most effective early years. Yet though he was born in Dublin, Carson had no alternative but to sacrifice his Irish unionism and abandon his fellow southern Unionists, when the tough decisions had to be made in 1913. By this stage power within unionism clearly rested with the Ulster bourgeoisie, and this new leadership was less interested in the concerns of southern Unionists. Perhaps it was inevitable that the regional and class differences, which unionism had done well to control, would ultimately split the movement. Therefore, a partitionist approach to the Irish question, which had its origins in the formation of the UUC in 1905, became widely canvassed and, by 1921, such a compromise appeared to many, both in Ireland and Britain, as the only practical solution. Though expedient, partition created new problems for the traditional minorities in Ireland, the northern Catholics and the southern Protestants.

The First World War damaged constitutional nationalism by delaying the implementation of Home Rule. At the same time, war encouraged violent nationalism. At Easter 1916, Fenians would seize the opportunity to strike a blow for Irish freedom, while British attention was firmly focused on the western front. The insurrectionists looked forward to the establishment of an independent Irish state, but they also looked back in seeing the 1916 rising as the latest in a sequence of rebellions. Hence, 1916 was intended to become part of the revolutionary nationalist tradition, with direct links to 1798, 1803, 1848 and 1867. Although the rising was a military failure, the political objectives of the leaders were partly met. They provoked a British response that was viewed by Irishmen as an overreaction. Consequently, a rebellion that was characterised by a lack of popular support in what might have been considered favourable circumstances, received a retrospective endorsement from the people. This was quickly translated into political support for Sinn Fein, which swept aside the IPP in the post-war general election. Thus, another objective of the insurrectionists, namely the obliteration of the IPP, was achieved. When the British refused to acknowledge the reality of the new situation in Ireland, a guerrilla war with the aim of forcing a British withdrawal ensued. Nationalism had undergone a process of radicalisation, but this too would pass. By the summer of 1921 both the British government and Sinn Fein were seeking to break the cycle of violence. In the negotiations which followed the truce, the Irish accepted dominion status, thereby putting the new Irish Free State on a constitutional par with Canada. Looking back from 1921, it is easy to assume that the collapse of the Union was inevitable, but this can be misleading.

The Union was not a success, and it eventually fell victim to the forces of revolutionary nationalism. Still, the fact that it lasted for 120 years suggests that it was not doomed from the outset. A legislative union had worked for Scotland and Wales, and both of these countries had a legacy of past conflict with England. Cultural nationalism had been particularly strong in Wales, but it did not develop into a political demand for Welsh independence. Yet, when cultural nationalism emerged in Ireland, it could not, despite the efforts of its early leaders, remain separate from political nationalism. Scotland had, of course, suffered terribly at the hands of the English in the eighteenth century. The unsuccessful attempt by 'Bonnie Prince Charlie's' Jacobite forces to seize the British Crown unleashed savage reprisals by the English government. In 1746, the remnants of the Jacobite army were slaughtered on Culloden Moor, and this was followed by the Highland clearances. The Scottish clan system was ruthlessly broken up, but this did not provoke a nationalist challenge to the 1707 Act of Union between England and Scotland. Instead, the Westminster government raised Highland regiments for the British army and this diverted the energies of the clansmen. More importantly, the government oversaw huge economic changes in Scotland, which raised the general standard of living and helped Scots to become assimilated into the United Kingdom, while retaining their strong sense of national identity.

This did not happen in Ireland. Here, there were obvious geographical complications, but this alone does not explain the failure to absorb the Irish into the United Kingdom. One obvious problem was the absence of industrialisation outside north-east Ulster. Ireland did not, therefore, enjoy her share of the spectacular economic growth that much of Britain experienced in the nineteenth century. While most economic historians are agreed that the Union was not a serious factor inhibiting Ireland's economic development, the perception among nationalists was very different. True, rapid industrialisation had also been confined to specific areas in Scotland and Wales, but the Irish experience was more complicated. The fact that northern Protestants enjoyed a near-monopoly of the economic benefits accruing from industrialisation did not go unnoticed by nationalists. More crucially, the economic downturn in mid-nineteenth century Ireland was in sharp contrast to developments in Britain, and the catastrophic impact of the famine further highlighted these differences.

In responding to all of these problems, the British offered too little, too late. The best example of this was Catholic emancipation. When it failed to appear as an addendum to the Act of Union, Catholics were presented with a clear grievance which, in time, they would seek to redress. Consequently, as far as the politically-conscious Catholic middle class was concerned, the Union operated with a clear Protestant bias. Indeed, the British government frequently found itself in a dilemma, caught between attempts to support a loyal Protestant minority and efforts to conciliate the less loyal Catholic majority. As the Catholic population was stereotyped as troublesome in this formative period, British policy consistently favoured the loyalists. In the end it took a colossal effort to gain Catholic emancipation, which had become a symbol for Catholic grievances in general. It was the struggle for emancipation that created the Catholic political nation. In the process Catholics ceased to be the passive people they had been at the time of the Union. Emancipation whetted Catholic appetites for further concessions, and new demands followed. Not surprisingly, Catholics believed that their suffering was due to their religion, and this provided a powerful impetus for the development of constitutional nationalism. Previously, nationalism had been the preserve of the politicised middle class, but the particular circumstances of the 1820s transformed it into a mass movement. More recent historical research has emphasised that O'Connell did not create a mass movement out of nothing. Instead, he led a Catholic nation already politicised and comfortable with the concept of collective action. Of course, this should not detract from O'Connell's contribution to constitutional nationalism, as he provided the inspirational leadership and direction for an increasingly confident and assertive Catholic bourgeoisie. Moreover, his political career was to have a powerful influence on contemporary European liberal thinking. Later, the emergence of a mass movement would be repeated in the last quarter of the nineteenth century, when the land issue mobilised the tenant farming class. Under O'Connell's leadership, Catholicism and nationalism became inseparable. This was a logical step, because O'Connell was quick to recognise that success in electoral politics required the active participation and support of the Catholic clergy.

Yet it is also important to stress the significance of Protestant nationalism, even though the numbers engaged were never large. O'Connell had a degree of Protestant support, while both the Young Irelanders in the 1840s and the early Home Rulers in the 1870s relied on Protestant leadership. A number of historians have suggested that the actions of this Protestant avant-garde within nationalism was an attempt by Protestants to stake a claim for leadership in a future Ireland, which had achieved some measure of freedom from Britain. Davis fitted this bill, as did Parnell. Under

Parnell's leadership nationalism, which had been in the doldrums since the early 1840s, recovered to become the dominant force in Irish politics. Indeed, the impact of the land agitation in 1879 marked a crucial turning point for constitutional nationalism. The Land League was the single most important movement in the development of nationalism. Unlike the Catholic Association, the Land League was a movement initiated by the masses, who had united in opposition to an alien landlord class, to redress the major economic grievance of land tenure.

Significantly, the Land League enjoyed success, because it operated both outside and inside Parliament. It also managed to build, in a very short time frame, a remarkable coalition of rural and semi-rural interests in a total membership approaching 200,000. Much of the Land League's dynamism and energy can be attributed to its grass roots leadership at local level. Essentially, these local leaders combined clear political objectives with their pursuit of the unifying goal of land ownership for Ireland's farmers. There was, of course, a good sprinkling of Fenian activists among this local leadership, and they clarified the link between major land reform and political freedom. Among the Fenian leaders who backed involvement in the League there was an assumption that a Westminster parliament would not desert its Irish landed brethren by transferring the ownership of property and that this would, therefore, bring the tenant farmers on board for a major drive towards independence. This did not transpire, however, and a new rural elite, including graziers, strong farmers, publicans, solicitors, shopkeepers and journalists, adopted a more cautious approach as it consolidated its economic and political power. After some hesitation, Parnell was awakened to the movement's potential, and he set out to control this new force and use it for his political ends. The land issue had mobilised the masses and, by linking the politics of Home Rule to the politics of land reform, Parnell won overwhelming popular support for a new style of constitutional nationalism. Both inside and outside Parliament, Parnell made this nationalism a confident, aggressive force, but the need to seek political allies at Westminster eventually smoothed nationalism's radical edge. Yet Parnell had succeeded in establishing a broad nationalist front, based on the fusion of agrarian and political forces. Although he was a conservative on social matters, the land agitation held out the prospect, at least for a brief period, of radical social change in Ireland. However, the tenant farmers who wanted to own their holdings did not support this. When the government facilitated this transfer of land ownership, nationalism also shed its radical social edge.

Moreover, Parnellism was effective because it embraced constitutional Fenianism. Even in 1886, when the limitations of a Home Rule settlement were finally exposed, constitutional separatists could take comfort from the belief that the door to full independence had been opened. The readiness with which separatists engaged in constitutional politics was neither surprising nor new. Conversely, throughout the century, mainstream nationalists often engaged in militant rhetoric while paying homage to Ireland's revolutionary tradition. On the other hand, revolutionary nationalism could feed off constitutional nationalism, as the Young Irelanders had done with the Repeal movement. There was, therefore, some overlap between constitutional and revolutionary nationalism, but it was the constitutional strain that proved much more powerful, a fact which the ultimate success of revolutionary nationalism in the 1916–21 period has obscured. Indeed, it may not even be accurate to speak of a revolutionary tradition in nineteenth century Ireland. Attempts by violent nationalists to secure Irish freedom were isolated and sporadic. Furthermore, the use of the term rebellion to describe the 1803 and 1848 incidents seems inappropriate given the small numbers involved and their negligible impact.

While the famine gave some impetus to revolutionary nationalism, this was most keenly felt among the Irish diaspora in the United States. The subsequent emergence of the Fenian movement on both sides of the Atlantic involved more serious preparation for revolutionary activity, though recent research has cast some doubt on the revolutionary commitment of the Fenian membership in Ireland. Yet revolutionary nationalist movements, particularly the Fenians, did raise the spectre of serious violence in Ireland or, even worse, Britain, if suitable concessions to Catholic nationalism were either rejected or delayed. The most effective nationalist leaders were those constitutionalists who understood how to milk this threat. One British statesman who took revolutionary nationalism seriously was Gladstone. Initially, he sought to remove its causes through a programme of social and economic improvements, but eventually came to the conclusion that only Home Rule would pacify Ireland. Believing that all other possibilities had been exhausted, Gladstone was prepared to split his party on Ireland, though he remained confident that the Irish could be assimilated like the Scots in the previous century. Of course, in his attempt to implement Irish Home

Rule, Gladstone was adamant that devolution would actually strengthen the Union. His big mistake, however, was to overlook the problem of Ulster.

The subsequent constitutional concessions made to Sinn Fein caused many members of the British establishment to rue the rejection of Gladstone's Home Rule Bills. The tenant farming class had prospered under constitutional nationalism, as the land problem had been resolved to their satisfaction. Indeed, the need to respond to the agitation of the United Irish League had been an important factor in the framing of the Wyndham Act. The Catholic middle class, particularly the business and commercial elements, had also benefited from the economic upturn in the last two decades of the nineteenth century, and they fully expected to play a prominent role in a Home Rule Ireland. These groups were not, to any real extent, interested in any possible cultural dimension of nationalism. Here, Ireland did not conform to the European pattern in which a cultural awakening preceded political nationalism. Instead, those who were drawn to cultural nationalism in Ireland rejected the process of modernisation welcomed by political nationalists. In fact, the pace of change towards the end of the century had caused upheaval and uncertainty within Irish society, a state of affairs that left one section of the people desperately searching for some kind of stability. Most of those who felt insecure as a result of these social, economic and cultural changes had not previously engaged with political nationalism, and this accounts for a new cadre of activists whose instinct was to stay aloof from conventional politics. Their dilemma was that Ireland did not have a rich cultural heritage to defend. This meant that much of their energy was spent on attacking English society and culture. In the end cultural nationalists had to come off their pedestal, as they were increasingly drawn towards more radical forms of political nationalism.

Unionism was slow to respond to the challenge of Parnellism, and it was only when Home Rule appeared imminent that it organised its parliamentary forces. However, once a decision was taken unionism took advantage of the building blocks already in place. To function as an effective political movement unionism welded together the Protestant forces of the Irish Conservative party, the Church of Ireland and the Orange Order. Initially, a significant body of Protestants had opposed the Union, but, as the century progressed, defence of the Union became increasingly bound to the Protestant interest. Undoubtedly, the impact of O'Connellism and the advance of the Catholic political nation had forced a reassessment of Protestant political thinking. Of course, O'Connell also presented a new electoral challenge, and it was the Tory response to O'Connellism that forged the essential element in the birth of unionism. For most of the nineteenth century pro-Union candidates enjoyed a majority of Irish representation, but the emergence of a Home Rule party in the last quarter of the nineteenth century decisively shifted the balance of power. Previously, the restricted franchise enabled pro-Union candidates to win seats all over Ireland, but the general elections of 1885–86 suddenly raised the Ulster profile of the Irish Unionist movement. In spite of its bleak electoral prospects, southern Unionists continued to play a prominent, and perhaps dominant, role within unionism until 1900. The influence of the landed class combined with Saunderson's leadership ensured that unionism remained an Irish phenomenon during this period. The landed influence also facilitated the alliance with British Conservatism, though, on both sides, this was essentially determined by political opportunism rather than ideology.

Naturally, the north's experience of industrialisation became a powerful feature of Ulster unionism, but the comfortable relationship between Irish landlordism and Ulster business during these early years tended to obscure any regional variation within unionism. A more self-reliant Ulster unionism did not emerge until after the bourgeois takeover of the leadership in the early years of the twentieth century. Unionism, moreover, cannot be dismissed as a purely negative movement. It was a complex coalition of different social groups and Protestant denominations held together by a common interest. In times of crisis the task of holding this coalition together was relatively straightforward, but class tensions quickly surfaced once the threat of Home Rule receded. To overcome this, unionism developed a populist rhetoric that made any compromise with nationalism unlikely. For the most part, moreover, Protestantism was an essential component of Ulster unionism, just as Catholicism was integral to the development of nineteenth century nationalism. It was perhaps ironic that, in time, Presbyterians who began the century as tentative converts to the Union had become its staunchest supporters by 1900. There were, of course, outstanding issues to be resolved, as Presbyterian tenant farmers continued to challenge their Church of Ireland landlords on the land issue, but these groups quickly put aside their differences once Home Rule threatened. At other times, however, these class tensions threatened to split

'Protestant' unionism, and the Orange Order became even more crucial through its role in holding together the pan-Protestant front at the heart of Ulster unionism. Indeed, the great success of unionism in this period was its ability to maintain this unity, both between the various Protestant classes and denominations, and between north and south.

*Chapter 9*
# Historiography

A**LL STUDENTS OF IRISH** history should be aware of the revisionist debate that really began with the appearance of *Irish Historical Studies* in the late 1930s, but reached a high point in the 1970s and 1980s when it was linked with political violence in Northern Ireland. In particular, a new generation of historians was keen to distance itself from what was seen as propaganda and violence which claimed a historical justification. As far as the nineteenth century was concerned, the revisionist debate was intensified by the publication of Roy Foster's book, *Modern Ireland 1600–1972*, in 1988. Foster was critical of the traditional nationalist understanding of the Irish past, and his work made an important contribution to the encouragement of new thinking on exploring Ireland's past. The book argues that the Union made little difference to Ireland and claims that the country was experiencing serious economic problems prior to the famine, leaving a large percentage of the population 'at risk'. After the famine Foster sees the growing power of the Catholic Church as a key development. It had been strengthened by the emergence of a dominant group of respectable or middling farmers and by the removal of the less devout cottier class. During this period Foster also dismisses the impact of rackrenting landlords and evictions in rural Ireland, describing how most farmers had enjoyed a rising standard of living up to the late 1870s. Subsequently, the political developments of the 1880s had the effect of intensifying sectarian feeling in Ulster. Later, the work of Foster and a number of other revisionist historians was attacked by a group of anti-revisionists led by Brendan Bradshaw and Seamus Deane, who accused the revisionists of undermining Ireland's nationalist icons, while excusing the British government for its failings, particularly the huge loss of life during the famine. However, none of these historians could dismiss Foster's simple claim that the Union 'formed the rhetorical issue of Irish politics: the thing to be for or against'.

The final years of the eighteenth century are analysed in SJ Connolly, *Divided Kingdom: Ireland 1630–1800* (Oxford, 2008). While he views the 1798 rebellion as a 'bloody civil war', Connolly stresses that it followed a long period of peace in Ireland in which 'day-to-day relations between Protestants and Catholics were becoming more relaxed', as Catholics were no longer regarded as a threat. Nevertheless, it was against this background that Defenderism emerged as a sophisticated ideology, which articulated new social and political aspirations in addition to the traditional grievances such as rents and tithes. This was partly due to the influence of ideas from France which introduced a new political language that combined an attack on privilege with the old idea of a 'people deprived of their lands and freedom by alien conquerors'. This Defender ideology reappeared with the Ribbon movement of the 1820s and 1830s. After the rebellion Connolly points out that most Catholics either supported the Union or were 'quietly neutral', and this allowed Pitt's government to invoke Catholic loyalism in the period from 1799–1800. Connolly concludes by suggesting that the Union was flawed and missed a great opportunity by abandoning the Catholic emancipation cause. Still, he is adamant that the Union had the virtue of 'lifting effective power out of the hands of the contending parties within Ireland' and was flexible enough to accommodate a series of major reforms in the nineteenth century. Significantly, Connolly rejects the argument that the Union was 'doomed to failure'. Subsequent revolutionary nationalism was only an intermittent minority movement, whereas the mainstream of Irish nationalism in the nineteenth century 'remained conspicuous above all for their willingness to negotiate a position for Irish Catholics within the structures of the British state'.

Grattan's impact on Irish politics in the run-up to the Union is assessed by Danny Mansergh, *Grattan's Failure: Parliamentary Opposition and the People in Ireland 1779–1800* (Dublin, 2005). Mansergh argues that there was a sharp increase in 'out-of-doors agitation' in the last two decades of the eighteenth century, and Grattan saw the events of 1782 as 'a popular revolution inspired by himself'. As the Catholic Committee's campaign for a Catholic Relief measure gathered pace in the early 1790s, there was a backlash from the Protestant Ascendancy, which shocked the British government in its scale and intensity. These pro-government Conservatives also used extra-parliamentary agitation in their determination to safeguard the Ascendancy class. Although pressure from Westminster had helped to produce the Catholic Relief Act in 1793, which enfranchised Catholics on the same basis as Protestants, Grattan continued to press for emancipation, but this was rejected by the Irish Parliament in May 1795. While Grattan had largely abandoned his strategy of public agitation with the threat of militant agitation by this stage, Mansergh rejects RB McDowell's contention that Grattan was the father of Irish liberalism. Rather, Mansergh argues, Grattan used a combination of parliamentary pressure supported by the implicit, or explicit, threat of force, which made him 'uncannily like Parnell'. In his conclusion Mansergh points out that historians remember Lord Clare as the architect of the Union, but he emphasises that Clare only espoused the Union as a reaction to 'the increasingly dangerous populist antics of competing factions within the Irish ruling class'.

A detailed study of the background to the Act of Union can be found in Patrick Geoghegan, *The Irish Act of Union: A Study in High Politics 1798–1801* (Dublin, 1999). Geoghegan's central argument is that a legislative union was Pitt's long-term goal and was not, therefore, an expedient response to rebellion. Moreover, his intention was to include a measure granting Catholic emancipation, as he assumed that such a move would bring stability to Ireland, but this was dropped under Clare's influence. In addressing the extent of corruption required to secure the bill's passage in the Irish Parliament, Geoghegan concludes that the extensive use of patronage was normal practice in contemporary Ireland and asserts that it was 'the use of generous patronage, borough compensation and the catholic question that secured a majority for the union'. In particular, the author notes that it was the enlistment of Catholic support for the Union that proved decisive, and he argues that promises were made to Irish Catholics that emancipation would follow a legislative union. Geoghegan then claims that emancipation became a victim of a constitutional struggle between Pitt and the monarchy, with George III being successful. When Pitt tried to force the issue in January 1801, the King viewed emancipation as a test of his constitutional powers, and he reacted in uncompromising style, meaning that a Catholic relief measure would have to be set aside while he remained on the throne. Essentially, Pitt had gambled on the weight of argument forcing George III into a U-turn, but, as Geoghegan describes, the Prime Minister, who had underestimated royal determination, subsequently pledged to drop the Catholic question, as he put the future security of the empire above all other political considerations.

Our understanding of Catholic politics in the early decades of the nineteenth century has been greatly enhanced by the work of Thomas Bartlett and Kevin Whelan. In *The Fall and Rise of the Irish Nation: The Catholic Nation, 1690–1830* (Dublin, 1992), Bartlett contends that while a union, from the British perspective, was desirable for imperial and commercial reasons and was made practicable because of the reaction to the 1798 rebellion, it was made necessary by 'the emergence of the Catholic question and the mobilisation and politicisation of the Catholic masses'. Whelan's later work, *The Tree of Liberty: Radicalism, Catholicism and the Construction of Irish Identity, 1760–1830* (Cork, 1996), supports Bartlett's view that Irish Catholics had undergone a process of politicisation which began in the 1790s. Both Bartlett and Whelan, therefore, challenge the view that O'Connell created the Catholic nation. Rather, they argue, O'Connell was in a position to take advantage of this development by the early 1820s, because, as Whelan claims, he benefited from the efforts of 'a very gifted generation of political activists, who were subsequently pushed aside as O'Connell asserted his authority. Bartlett highlights the contribution of the Catholic bourgeoisie, mainly merchants, who dominated Catholic politics. Their 'awareness of the power of the masses beneath them' helped to produce a new Catholic consciousness in the early years of the nineteenth century. Bartlett also emphasises the importance of secret societies, particularly the Ribbonmen, in the first two decades of the nineteenth century. These societies advanced the process of politicisation through the identification of grievances and by their actions to redress these grievances, which brought them face to face with the British state. Particular attention is paid to the 1826 Waterford by-election and the pivotal role played by Thomas Wyse, allowing Bartlett to stress that the events of 1826, when the electoral power of the landlords was spectacularly broken, 'revealed the presence of an aggressively politicised Catholic nation, one whose identity had been formed by opposition to Protestantism and by hostility from Protestants'. Whelan contrasts the inclusiveness of the United Irishmen with O'Connell's Catholic nationalism, suggesting that 'he was unable, or disinclined to create a nationalist movement that could transcend his Catholic support base'.

O'Connell's earlier influence on the evolution of the emancipation campaign is dealt with by Fergus O'Ferrall, *Catholic Emancipation: Daniel O'Connell and the Birth of Irish Democracy* (Dublin, 1985). O'Ferrall notes that from 1808 O'Connell had 'almost single-handedly' prevented Irish Catholic opinion from accepting any form of qualified emancipation, as he demanded full emancipation with no state interference in appointments to the Catholic hierarchy. Moreover, he points to O'Connell's brilliance in attracting a coalition of interests in the Catholic Association. During 1823–24, O'Connell developed his more strident approach to Irish agitation which attracted the masses, but he was astute enough to recognise that the Association's success would depend on retaining the support of the wealthy middle class and the cautious Catholic gentry for the agitation. O'Ferrall also highlights the pressure placed on the Association by O'Connell to focus on the peasantry's grievances, particularly tithes, and he shows how O'Connell deliberately raised expectations of the benefits that would follow emancipation. In analysing the importance of O'Connell's Clare by-election success in 1828, O'Ferrall is adamant that the victory opened 'a new epoch in Irish politics and in Anglo-Irish relations', and he contends that Peel certainly regarded the Clare success as a real turning point. Furthermore, in granting emancipation in 1829, the author claims that the Wellington-Peel administration had 'defused a potentially revolutionary situation'. Peel's real concerns, of course, were for the Church of Ireland, the landlord class and the ultimate safety of the Union. O'Ferrall concludes by praising the Catholic Church which had committed itself to a great popular political struggle. Elsewhere in Europe, the church became a consistent opponent of liberalism. Nevertheless, O'Ferrall acknowledges that the focus on Catholic grievances, which was the key aspect of politicisation in the 1820s, gave Irish nationalism a sectarian base and deepened the divisions between the 'two peoples on the island'. Patrick Geoghegan, *King Dan: The Rise of Daniel O'Connell, 1775–1829* (Dublin, 2008), states that while O'Connell had never abandoned his religion to become a King's Counsel or MP, he actually only became a devout Catholic in 1826. Significantly, O'Connell believed that the Catholic religion helped to define an Irishman and gave him 'a sense of identity and a sense of inferiority'. Geoghegan adds that O'Connell recognised that this 'culture of defeat' had to be challenged and that the Irish had to learn 'to fight the establishment on its own terms, to bully, to intimidate, to refuse to be cowed'.

Gustave de Beaumont, *Ireland: Social, Political, and Religious* (London,

2006), presents a contemporary view of O'Connell's political impact following an extensive tour undertaken by the author in 1839. De Beaumont was particularly impressed by O'Connell's authority over the masses, describing constitutional agitation as a middle way 'between legal opposition and revolt'. He also claimed that O'Connell understood the advantages to be gained 'from the shelter of the law, and how far violence may be pushed without passing its limits'. De Beaumont attributed all of Ireland's problems to 'a bad aristocracy' and argued that the best hope of progress and improvement lay with the Whig party. He was adamant, moreover, that nothing could be achieved in Ireland without the involvement of the Catholic Church. Significantly, he also commented on the differences between Ulster, which was more prosperous, and the rest of Ireland, arguing that in the north 'there is more political than social misery; whereas in the rest of Ireland, there is more social misery than political'. Ulster's reluctance to engage with O'Connellism is examined in an important essay by SJ Connolly, 'Mass politics and sectarian conflict, 1823–30' which appears in *A New History of Ireland V: Ireland under the Union I, 1801–70* (Oxford, 1989) edited by WE Vaughan. Connolly rejects the traditional argument that it was Protestantism that determined Ulster's lack of support for the emancipation campaign. Rather, he suggests, the Catholic population in the north was concentrated among the lower social orders. These labourers and cottiers had other concerns, and their poor levels of literacy ensured that the spread of political consciousness struggled to penetrate Catholic Ulster. Connolly also observes that most of the money contributed to the Catholic rent did not come in pennies but in shillings and pounds. The majority of contributors, moreover, were the artisans, shopkeepers and professional and business classes in the towns. In his analysis of the Catholic Association Connolly argues that one of its great achievements was to present itself 'not as the exemplars of a new style of democratic and constitutional agitation, but as the champions of an oppressed Irish Catholicism'. O'Connell's principal biographer, Oliver MacDonagh, *O'Connell: The Life of Daniel O'Connell, 1775–1847* (London, 1991), offers a detailed analysis of his subject's political career, emphasising that the clergy had no role in the early days of the Catholic Association, but O'Connell changed this to make the movement a success. He then describes that the decision to collect the 'rent' outside churches on Sundays was a brilliant idea, as it caught those with no houses of their own. (The large number of domestic servants in Ireland usually lived in the homes of their employers). MacDonagh also analyses the importance of the role played by the clergy in the Catholic Association, noting that parish priests, who had their subscriptions waived, played the crucial role in rural areas where no committees existed, making the church 'the main engine of fund-raising'. Following the emancipation victory, however, MacDonagh points out that the lower clergy were warned by the bishops to refrain from any further political activity. O'Connell's success as the leader of constitutional nationalism was due, in part, to his pragmatic, flexible approach. MacDonagh contrasts the 'popular style', which he used in Ireland, with the 'political style' that he would deploy at Westminster. Here, the defeat of the repeal motion in 1834 allowed O'Connell to develop better relations with the Whigs, which facilitated the establishment of the Whig alliance. On the popular campaign for repeal, MacDonagh explains that O'Connell only shifted the scene of operations to Ireland following the Tory victory in the general election of July 1841. The movement that subsequently developed was in MacDonagh's view 'a prototype Sinn Fein'. While the author notes that O'Connell's first political speech opposed the Union, his address at the launch of the Loyal National Repeal Association in July 1840 demanded 'Full Justice or Repeal', and this leads MacDonagh to suggest that the primary purpose of the repeal campaign was to force reforms from a reluctant government in London.

Three important general histories of the period, Foster, *Modern Ireland*, Paul Bew, *Ireland: The Politics of Enmity 1798–2006* (Oxford, 2007) and Alvin Jackson, *Ireland 1798–1998: Politics and War* (Oxford, 1999) are each, to varying degrees, critical of O'Connell's leadership. Foster contends that O'Connellism reinforced the sectarian nature of Irish politics, while Bew questions O'Connell's liberal, democratic reputation. On the veto question he went against Thomas Moore and Richard Lalor Sheil, the leading Catholic liberals and, having achieved emancipation, Bew describes O'Connell's failure to maintain a working relationship with liberal Presbyterianism in the north. In 1845 O'Connell adopted a sectarian stance on the university question to the dismay of the Young Ireland movement, and Bew also reveals that in private correspondence with Archbishop Cullen in 1842 O'Connell claimed that repeal would destroy Protestantism in Ireland. Jackson views O'Connell as a mixture of a conviction politician and an opportunist. While he concedes that O'Connell's .contribution to constitutional nationalism is beyond question, he claims that the Irish leader was essentially a product of the penal era and failed to rise above the 'peculiarly bitter sectarian feeling' present in nineteenth-century Irish politics. In analysing his handling of the emancipation and repeal issues, Jackson provides a convincing argument, suggesting that emancipation was a goal that was pursued with ruthless conviction, while repeal was a sincere conviction, but one that only tended to surface when all other political avenues had been blocked. DG Boyce, *Nationalism in Ireland* (London, 1982) and *Nineteenth-Century Ireland: The Search for Stability* (Dublin, 1990), highlights O'Connell's sincere belief that Catholics could become 'loyal subjects' of the United Kingdom if their grievances were redressed. While O'Connell always regarded repeal as 'the highest bid that he could make', he also viewed the Union as 'a real and lasting possibility'. Moreover, as Boyce claims, the fact that O'Connell identified Catholic with nationalist does not brand him a bigot. Certainly, his rhetoric was sometimes sectarian in tone but, as Boyce describes, Protestants had sought 'to frustrate every political move he had made throughout his career', concluding that 'O'Connell can hardly be blamed for the religious divisions of Ireland, or the political algebra commonly practised in that country'. Furthermore, the core of the O'Connellite movement was not the Catholic clergy but the educated middle class cadre of leaders, and its power was based on its mass appeal which, Boyce argues, was largely due to O'Connell's attributes as a brilliant orator and commanding personality. A much older, but still useful, general survey, JC Beckett, *The Making of Modern Ireland, 1603–1923* (London, 1966), argues that O'Connell's use of violent rhetoric was deliberately calculated, as he was intent in setting an example of 'fearless defiance' of the state. This drew a repressive response from the authorities which won further support for the O'Connellite cause in England. Following emancipation, O'Connell retained his ability to rouse the peasantry. Beckett sees this as his greatest strength, but notes that O'Connell could not organise an effective political campaign without the support of the middle class whose main interest was in reform. Although repeal was his ultimate goal, Beckett explains that this is why he deviated between repeal and reform.

Jackson and Boyce also consider the impact made by the Independent Opposition party in the 1850s. While Jackson urges caution in making comparisons between the Independents and the later Home Rule party, he notes that the Independents were first to exercise influence while holding the balance of power in the House of Commons. Like the Parnellites, moreover, the Independents were prepared to back the Tories in preference to the Whigs if this offered a temporary advantage, and, like the Home Rulers, the Independents lost ground during periods of 'relative agrarian tranquillity or prosperity'. Crucially, however, Jackson is adamant that the Independent Opposition party was 'not nationalist in any meaningful sense', and it suffered through the absence of a national organisation which could act as an electoral machine. This was a major departure from both the O'Connellite and Parnellite eras. Boyce doubts that the Independent Opposition party was ever an effective political force, adding that the problems it faced were instructive for all political parties in Ireland under the Union. What was required was mass support and the imposition of strict party discipline, neither of which featured during the 1850s. Another important historian who sheds light on political developments in nineteenth-century Ireland is KT Hoppen, *Ireland since 1800: Conflict and Conformity* (London, 1989) and *Elections, Politics and Society in Ireland, 1832–1885* (Oxford, 1984). Hoppen observes O'Connell's recognition of the fact that mass support for emancipation was based on the assumption that it would lead directly to a series of economic benefits including lower rents. In particular, he argues that local affairs and local grievances, rather than national issues, were more important in determining political participation and the scale of mobilisation.

Historians continue to debate the wider issues associated with the famine. Two writers who consider government policy during the tragedy are Donal Kerr, *A Nation of Beggars? Priests, People and Politics in Famine Ireland 1846–1852* (Oxford, 1994) and Peter Gray, *Famine, Land and Politics: British Government and Irish Society 1843–50* (Dublin, 1999). Kerr examines the relationship between Lord John Russell's Whig government and the Catholic Church and details the enormous pressure put on the hierarchy from both the lower clergy and individuals, as the tragedy unfolded. Gray looks, more specifically, at the impact of ideology on the administration's decision-making process, concluding that 'providentialism' exerted a powerful influence on key figures who were responsible for the British government's handling of the crisis. In particular, Gray argues that a belief that the blight was dispatched by God 'to bring Ireland into a higher state of social and moral organisation through a necessary measure of pain', shaped contemporary attitudes and subsequent apologetics'. A more scathing attack on the British government's response to the crisis is found in Christine Kinealy, *The Great Irish Famine: Impact, Ideology and Rebellion* (London, 2002). Kinealy argues forcefully that British culpability for the suffering should not be forgotten, and she questions the contention which emphasises the continuity between the pre-famine and post-famine periods, rejecting the view that a major Irish famine was inevitable. The economic historian, Cormac O'Grada, *The Great Irish Famine* (Dublin, 1989), presents a series of economic statistics to highlight Ireland's economic progress prior to the famine. When this is added to the unlikelihood of a succession of harvest failures like those of the late 1840s, O'Grada concludes that it is hardly surprising that both the Irish people and the British government were shocked at the speed and scale of the catastrophe. Previously, Joel Mokyr, *Why Ireland Starved: An Analytical and Quantitative History of the Irish Economy, 1800–1850* (London, 1985), saw famine as a likely consequence of the population explosion in the early decades of the nineteenth century. Mokyr also contrasts the £10.5 million spent by the British government on famine relief with the hopeless outlay of £69.3 million on the Crimean War. James S Donnelly, *The Great Irish Potato Famine* (Stroud, 2001), casts much of the blame for the catastrophe on the Irish landlords, a view widely shared in contemporary Britain, concluding that the world's richest nation should not have allowed one million people to die in its own 'backyard'. In March 1847 almost 50,000 Irish immigrants arrived in Liverpool. Many actually died on the streets, and this was widely reported in British newspapers, which accused Irish landlords of evading their responsibilities and shifting the problem onto the British taxpayer. Donnelly also notes that having spent nearly £10 million on famine relief by the spring of 1847, with little sign of real improvement, many Britons came to view the problem as racial or cultural, rather than financial, and this strengthened the opinion articulated in *The Times* that the Irish were 'a nation of beggars'. Recently, our understanding of the famine has benefited from numerous local studies. A good example is an essay by Matthew Stout which appears in Chris Morash and Richard Hayes (eds), *Fearful Realities: New Perspectives on the Famine* (Dublin, 1996). Stout's essay, 'The Geography and Implications of Post-Famine Population Decline in Baltyboys, County Wicklow', examines one major estate in Wicklow during and after the famine. On this estate, consolidation, and by implication depopulation, was a pre-famine objective of the Smiths, the estate owners. Here, the landless cottier and the smaller tenants could not survive the loss of their staple food and the decreased demand for their labour. Stout comments that on the Smith estate, 'largely due to the efforts of the resident landlord and his remarkable wife', this group emigrated rather than died. Another essay in the same volume by Robert Mahony, 'Historicising the Famine: John Mitchel and the Prophetic Voice of Swift', records Mitchel's outrage at O'Connell's refusal to link repeal and the famine. His failure to make such a connection cost O'Connell the support of the suffering Irish poor, 'whose inevitably short-term interest in survival rendered O'Connell's style of political action irrelevant'. A more in-depth study of the detail of landlord-tenant relations during the famine is presented by Desmond Norton, *Landlords, Tenants, Famine: The Business of an Irish Land Agency in the 1840s* (Dublin, 2006). The biggest Irish land agents at the time, Stewart and Kincaid, only contemplated eviction as a last resort. Indeed, as Norton describes, some landlords invested considerable sums on their estates during the 1840s. The future Prime Minister, Viscount Palmerston, had lands in North Sligo, and he spent money on improvement – draining bogs, building harbours, reseeding land, making new roads, building both Protestant and Catholic schools and constructing a parochial house at Mullaghmore. While he was slow to respond to the famine, Palmerston subsequently spent about £6,000 on assisted emigration. Norton also stresses that Ireland had a genuine cash economy, much more than has hitherto been assumed, before the famine. Tenants sold produce at fairs to raise cash, and there were 270 such fairs in County Clare alone in 1845. On the key question of evictions, Norton argues that it is very difficult to produce accurate figures, but he rejects the common argument that landlords and their agents were uncaring. Rather, he contends, they were, for the most part, progressive and humane, though he adds that the initiative for many of the improvements undertaken by landlords actually came from the land agents.

The most authoritative commentary on landlord-tenant relations in the period immediately after the famine is WE Vaughan, *Landlords and Tenants in mid-Victorian Ireland* (Oxford, 1994). Vaughan estimates that there were 70,000 evictions in the period from 1846–53, though the uneven nature of these meant that some counties were hit particularly hard. On the relationship between land and politics, Vaughan analyses the link between a political breakthrough and an economic crisis, concluding that the essential difference between the agrarian problems of the early 1860s and those of the late 1870s was that an effective group of leaders, particularly Parnell and Davitt, emerged to exploit the latter crisis. This had not happened in the 1860s, and this particular economic downturn, therefore, failed to develop a powerful political dimension. In his analysis of the land issue Paul Bew, *Land and National Question in Ireland 1858–1882* (Dublin, 1979), highlights the remarkable coalition of agrarian classes that came together in 1879. Naturally, this added to the Land League's influence, but Bew notes that from 1880 on tension emerged between these social classes with the graziers and strong farmers quickly becoming the dominant force in agrarian politics. In his recent, *The Politics of Enmity*, Bew sees Parnell's participation in the land struggle as an attempt to attract younger, more progressive landlords to the emerging Home Rule movement, as this would give constitutional nationalism 'sufficient social cachet' with a Westminster Parliament that was still dominated by the landed influence. Furthermore, Bew views Parnell's decision to engage with the land struggle as a huge political gamble for a young Protestant landlord. With only just over four years experience as an MP, the 32-year old Parnell was risking his future political career, and this explains his hesitation in committing himself to the Land League. Once on board, however, Parnell immediately displayed the political instincts which made him such an effective leader of nationalism. Bew notes that Gladstone, who had known both men, much preferred O'Connell to Parnell. Although Parnell was regarded as a ruthless political operator, Bew is, nevertheless, adamant that he never accepted the revolutionary premises of his Fenian supporters. Rather, he argues, Parnell was a conservative nationalist who sought to reconcile landlordism and nationalism by campaigning for major land reforms that would be acceptable both to Protestant landlords and Catholic tenants. This would, of course, allow members of the Protestant gentry, like himself, to play a leading role in any future Home Rule assembly. With an eye on future political developments, Bew notes that the Kilmainham treaty was the first occasion when a British Prime Minister sought to bring on board the political leadership of a violent nationalist organisation (Land League) by a process of 'secret negotiation and concession'. While Jackson accuses O'Connell of failing to rise above the sectarianism so prevalent in contemporary politics, he suggests that Parnell alone among nineteenth-century Irish leaders had the capacity to overcome the sectarianism rooted in Irish society.

Three essays by Vincent Comerford, which appear in WE Vaughan (ed),

*A New History of Ireland VI: Ireland Under the Union II, 1870–1921* (Oxford, 1996), provide a sharp analysis of nationalist Ireland during the Parnellite period. While Butt's fledgling Home Rule movement was obviously not separatist, Fenians, who had become weary of the shackles imposed by Charles Kickham, viewed the new organisation as a step in the right direction. Comerford emphasises that Fenian activists subsequently played a prominent role during elections and were more important than the clergy, whose main involvement was in the selection of parliamentary candidates. Memorably, Comerford describes Parnell's political style as creating the impression that he was prepared for anything while committing himself to nothing. This is what attracted the support of Devoy and the Fenians. In the New Departure, Davitt and Devoy assumed that they were launching a radical revolution, but Parnell, who was thought to be in support of such a venture, quickly asserted his authority. A recent study, Richard English, *Irish Freedom: The History of Nationalism in Ireland* (London, 2006) develops this theme, suggesting that Parnell's legacy can be claimed by both moderates and extremists, which partly explains his wide ranging appeal. English sees Parnell as a London-based politician dependent on Irish-based power, and as a parliamentarian who used the implicit threat of extra-parliamentary muscle. Jackson, *Home Rule: An Irish History 1800–2000* (London, 2003), argues that Parnell was not a great thinker or innovator in the Butt mould, but he was a 'skilful opportunist' who was able to take advantage of the Fenian initiative in the land struggle. Later, the formation of the National League in 1882 gave Parnell much more control of the nationalist movement and harnessed the power of the Catholic Church in a manner that was reminiscent of the O'Connell era. Jackson also demonstrates that Parnell favoured cooperation with the Conservative party on the Home Rule question and that he hid his contempt for Gladstone. On the broader issue of cooperation between the constitutional and revolutionary wings of nationalism, Jackson acknowledges that tension frequently arose between the constitutionalists and the militants, but both groups clearly understood the importance of national unity which could advance both sets of aims. In his assessment of the growing power of the Home Rule party, Alan O'Day, *Irish Home Rule 1867–1921* (Manchester, 1998), shows how electoral reform and redistribution played into the party's hands by abolishing small borough seats, thereby strengthening the party's rural orientation.

TW Moody, *Davitt and the Irish Revolution 1846–82* (Oxford, 1982), examines the Land League's relationship with the Catholic Church and stresses that the Mayo Land League had to cope with initial hostility from many bishops in the west. However, the lower clergy, particularly the curates, quickly became involved, and this, together with the movement's early success in attracting members, soon forced a change of mind by the hierarchy who feared that they might jeopardise the church's influence in rural Ireland. Moody's contention that Davitt was the prime mover in promoting cooperation between Fenians and constitutionalists to campaign for self-government in tandem with radical land reform is challenged by Laurence Marley, *Michael Davitt: Freelance Radical and Frondeur* (Dublin, 2007). Marley gives the credit to Clan na Gael and also notes that Davitt claimed to be the instigator of the Irishtown meeting in April 1879, when the real organiser was the editor of the *Connaught Telegraph*, James Daly. Marley later takes issue with Bew's argument that Parnell engaged with the land question in an attempt to reconcile landlordism and nationalism. In Marley's view, this ignores the extent to which the pragmatic Parnell had alienated his own class during the Land War with his repeated attacks on landlordism. The fall of Parnell is carefully analysed by Frank Callanan, *The Parnell Split* (Cork, 1992) and *TM Healy* (Cork, 1996). Parnell's appeal to the 'hillside men' following his break with the party was a predictable and logical move, because Parnell was, in Callanan's opinion, basing his strategy on the old premise that if constitutional nationalism could not make headway, then revolutionary nationalism would take its place. Moreover, as Callanan argues, only Parnell had the capacity to retain Fenian support for the constitutional movement and, by definition therefore, only Parnell had the ability to control Fenianism.

The two most important works on land and politics are Donald Jordan, *Land and Politics in Ireland: County Mayo from the Plantation to the Land War* (Cambridge, 1994) and Philip Bull, *Land, Politics and Nationalism: A study of the Irish Land Question* (Dublin, 1996). While the main focus of Bull's work is William O'Brien's United Irish League, he argues that such was the strength of the consolidation of the land and national questions in the last three decades of the nineteenth century that the separation of the two issues was impossible in practice. In stressing that the land struggle is better understood as a feature running from 1879–1903, Bull describes how participation in agrarian politics gave the IPP a social base. The significance of the Boer War is emphasised as Bull suggests that the conflict was the main reason for the UIL's rapid spread outside its western base. In Connacht, meanwhile, the involvement of the Catholic clergy ensured that the new movement won the support of the more moderate members of local society. Jordan's in-depth look at the dynamics of the conflict in County Mayo demonstrates that it was the issue of rents that brought 'the various farming cultures' together in 1879. The agrarian struggle was led by a new political elite, comprising professional men, shopkeepers and strong farmers, which operated 'in defiance of priests and landlords' during the early days of the Land War. Jordan concludes by suggesting that there were two simultaneous agrarian revolutions in Ireland between 1879 and 1882: 'one by large graziers who wanted to be free of rents and landlords so that they could fully profit from the market, and one by small farmers who wanted protection from eviction'.

Looking at the Home Rule issue from the Westminster perspective the work of three historians stands out. JL Hammond, *Gladstone and the Irish Nation* (London, 1938), remains an important source. Arguing that the Irish problem was the dominant issue for Gladstone towards the end of his political career, Hammond points to the Liberal leader's opinion that if Westminster failed to remedy Irish grievances, then the Union could not be maintained in its present form. In addition, the author notes that in a series of speeches on the Irish problem during 1882–83 Gladstone did not dismiss Home Rule out of hand and preferred to focus on the practical difficulties of devolution. Hammond also explains Gladstone's refusal to consider Ulster Protestant opposition to Home Rule in 1886, because he felt that the minority requiring protection was the landlord class, not Ulster Protestants. The Liberal Prime Minister viewed Ireland through a European lens, and he thought that British statesmen could not condemn examples of Austrian and Russian oppression while failing to govern Ireland properly. More recently, EF Biagini, *British Democracy and Irish Nationalism 1876–1906* (Cambridge, 2007), rejects the traditional argument that Gladstone's support for Home Rule split his party, cost it working class support and contributed to its ultimate demise. Instead, Biagini contends that Home Rule 'fired the public imagination of the peoples of the United Kingdom' and proved to be popular with the newly enfranchised masses. In considering Home Rule Biagini argues forcefully that Gladstone's principal objective was to preserve the Union. To achieve this Gladstone was prepared to think outside the box and introduce all sorts of reforms including Home Rule. James Loughlin, *Gladstone, Home Rule and the Ulster Question 1882–93* (Dublin, 1986), stresses that Gladstone was one of the few British statesmen in the nineteenth century, who had a real grasp of Irish history. He also gives considerable weight to Gladstone's obsession with justice and his distaste for coercion. Nevertheless, Loughlin points out that Gladstone saw a Home Rule solution to the Irish problem in conservative terms, as he hoped that the landlord class could return as the natural political leaders in a new Dublin assembly. Thus, it was clear that Gladstone regarded a Home Rule parliament as the best barrier to the revival of revolutionary nationalism.

The impact made by revolutionary nationalism over the course of the nineteenth century is considered in a number of the important general works. Foster does not dismiss Emmet as a dreamer who took his place among revolutionary Irish martyrs. Indeed, he describes a highly professional operative who had significant support among the artisan class in Dublin and other Irish towns. The rebellion of Young Ireland extremists in 1848 proved to be influential, not for what it achieved but, as Foster indicates, for the way in which it was interpreted. Jackson notes that Emmet sought to rekindle the flame of militant republicanism, but his actions in 1803 'subverted his professed ideals', as it fuelled sectarianism in Irish politics and undermined the demand for Catholic relief. Later, Jackson claims that the militancy of the Young Irelanders was 'both fired and destroyed' by the famine. Bew describes Emmet as a man of 'considerable idealism and drive', but he was undermined by government agents, poor communications and poorer explosives. In his analysis of the 1848 rising, Bew argues that 'Young Irelanders were lost when they attempted to spread revolution to the countryside, as long as the Catholic clergy remained opposed'. There was bitter hostility towards Britain as a result of the famine, but this did not translate into support for the Young Ireland rebels.

In his analysis of Fenianism Foster suggests that it created a 'mentality', rather than acted as a genuine revolutionary movement. Fenianism captured the imagination and could arouse great sympathy, as was evident at the funeral of Terence Bellew MacManus. Leaning on the work of Tom Garvin, *Nationalist Revolutionaries in Ireland 1858–1928* (Oxford, 1987), Foster stresses that Fenianism was representative of the petty bourgeois class. For a secret organisation operating within a tight cell structure, Fenianism's impact on the public was remarkable. However, as Foster contends, the dilemma for Fenianism was the choice between the temptation to use the land issue to mobilise support for political goals, or to refuse to dilute their simple physical force nationalist principles, and this tension was further reflected among Fenianism's American supporters. After the failure of the Fenian rising, Foster argues that the movement's strength remained 'moral and passive', and it helped to make the language of republican separatism 'respectable' in Ireland. Jackson emphasises that, from the outset, Fenianism, unlike the Young Ireland movement, was dedicated to producing a revolution. Indeed, Garvin had previously suggested that Stephens was prompted to take action in the 1850s, because he sensed that post-famine Irish society was developing in a way which was hostile to revolution. This rendered the work of a revolutionary elite even more important. From its inception, therefore, the Fenian movement was preparing to seize any opportunity to launch a revolution if Britain found herself engaged in a foreign war, and Jackson suggests that such a military distraction appeared to be on the cards in the 1850s and 1860s. Certainly, many of the Fenian leaders who had experienced periods of exile in France, America and even Australia were 'sensitive to the international scene'. Jackson describes how Fenianism responded successfully to developments in post-fame society. This involved the further development of towns and increased numbers among the ranks of the petty bourgeoisie. Indeed, Fenianism made most appeal to artisans, shop assistants, travelling salesmen and farmers' sons, the group which felt most hampered by social and political constraints. Moreover, as Jackson insists, the fact that it had attracted 54,000 recruits by 1864, proves that Fenianism had more than superficial appeal. For these recruits the social outlet, the use of ranks and the involvement in 'war games' allowed Jackson to draw a comparison with the UVF in 1913–14. The other key point highlighted by Jackson is the shift away from deference associated with the Fenian movement. Fenians refused to defer to landlords or the clergy, though Richard English argues that while the movement was anti-clerical in theory, the fact that most Fenians were practising Catholics ruled out the possibility of Fenianism becoming wholly secular. Paul Bew, in turn, emphasises the international dimension of Fenianism, claiming that the movement's formation proved that 'a greater Ireland beyond the seas now existed'. At home, he states that reports of the growing rural hardship of the early 1860s stimulated the movement's early growth, and he records that Fenianism was in favour of radical agrarian objectives, though these objectives were only thought to be attainable after freedom had been won. In particular, Bew illustrates the *Irish People's* frequent attacks on the grazier class and its repeated exhortations to reconquer the land for the people. Bew also focuses on Archbishop Cullen's opposition to Fenianism, stating that he was sometimes critical of the British government 'for treating the movement too leniently'. Certainly, the Clerkenwell bombing had caused widespread panic in the capital, leading to the recruitment of 50,000 special constables within a month, and Bew describes how the attack opened up divisions over Irish policy between the two main parties at Westminster.

Of the more specialist books, two deserve mention: Vincent Comerford, *The Fenians in Context: Irish Politics and Society 1842–1882* (Dublin, 1985) and Owen McGee, *The IRB: The Irish Republican Brotherhood from the Land League to Sinn Fein* (Dublin, 2005). Comerford's work asks if Fenianism should even be regarded as a genuine revolutionary movement. Instead, he regards participation in activities, particularly drill, as a 'social rather than purely military' experience. Indeed, he suggests that for the movement to recruit and retain members it had to go outside the narrow confines of physical force nationalism and engage in more mundane pursuits such as the organisation of sporting and leisure pursuits. McGee also questions Fenianism's claim to an instrument of revolutionary ambition by arguing that its real purpose was political. It sought to develop political consciousness in an attempt to prepare the country and its people for independence. In particular, McGee stresses that the Fenians were intent on advancing democratic ideals and sought to break the power of elites in Ireland. He also chronicles the prominent role played by Fenian activists such as Thomas Brennan, Matt Harris, Michael Boyton and PJ Sheridan in the Land League. For McGee, it was the influence of these local Fenians and others that helped to transform the Land League into such a powerful, national movement.

In examining cultural nationalism English argues that Davis sought to build an Irish nation that transcended religious and ethnic differences by highlighting its distinctive culture. Bew also comments on Davis's ability to break out of the religious straitjacket, when he states that 'Davis had, uniquely in Irish politics, a gift for holding and making friends across divides'. Jackson sees Davis and his fellow Young Irelanders as 'strongly elitist'. Like Parnell, Jackson notes that Davis wanted to win over the Protestant gentry to the cause of nationality. While O'Connell was a practical agitator, Davis was a nationalist theoretician who, nevertheless, acted as a 'moderating influence among Young Irelanders'. Foster, who regards Davis as the 'purest Irish patriot', describes how he adopted the 'necessarily pluralist ideology' of the Irish-Protestant nationalist, though, in the end, Davis's celebration of Irish history necessitated his support for Catholic nationalism. Previously, as Foster states, the Young Irelanders worked together to advance the history of 'a racial community struggling against foreign domination', which tended to stress the 'romance' of violent resistance to English oppression. Although Davis stressed the importance of the Irish language, Foster makes the important point that Young Ireland ideas were disseminated more widely because they were expressed in English. In assessing the impact made by the Gaelic League, Foster claims that the identification of Catholicism with Gaelic culture became inevitable. League activists, among whom former emigrants were prominent, viewed the remnants of Gaelic civilisation in the west as the way ahead for cultural nationalists, but, as Foster records, their belief that this cultural revival should remain above politics was not solely due to the influence of Protestant leaders such as Hyde. Contrasting the camps led Hyde and Yeats, Foster sees the Gaelic League as 'respectable, suburban and bourgeois', whereas the Anglo-Irish literary avant-garde was closed and elitist.

The major study of cultural nationalism remains John Hutchinson, *The Dynamics of Cultural Nationalism: The Gaelic Revival and the Creation of the Irish Nation State* (London, 1987). Hutchinson argues that the aim of cultural nationalists to stay above politics was unrealistic, and he details the tensions among Gaelic League members, as the intellectuals such as Hyde objected to the movement's growing identification with sectarian or separatist causes. He also claims that the Gaelic League and the GAA were not really part of a genuine cultural revival, as both movements were essentially engaged in the 'invention' of traditions for Ireland. Two later works, Senia Paseta, *Before the Revolution: Nationalism, Social Change and Ireland's Catholic Elite, 1879–1922* (Cork, 1999) and Patrick Maume, *The Long Gestation: Irish Nationalist Life 1891–1918* (Dublin, 1999), agree that neither cultural nor separatist nationalism made any real impact on the Catholic elite around the turn of the century. Indeed, Maume suggests that the Gaelic League initially attracted a significant number of Protestants and Unionists, 'who saw language revival as non-political or who hoped that cultural revivalism might replace political nationalism'. He also presents the view that many of the League's attitudes were anathema to those with Fenian sympathies, thus challenging the argument that a merger between cultural nationalism and political separatism was inevitable. Maume, who views Moran as a follower of O'Connell, whereas Callanan sees him in the Healy mould, claims that Moran saw the key struggle as between Catholic and Protestant, rather than between Ireland and Britain. A new work on the GAA, Mike Cronin, William Murphy and Paul Rouse (eds), *The Gaelic Athletic Association 1884-2009* (Dublin, 2009), commemorates the 125th anniversary of the organisation. In this collection of important essays, Cronin shows that the early leaders, such as Cusack and Davin, never just regarded the GAA as a straightforward sporting body that would restrict itself to purely sporting activities. Instead, they intended that the GAA 'would underpin parallel efforts elsewhere to create an Irish culture'.

The most important historian working on the evolution of unionism in the nineteenth century is Alvin Jackson. While organised unionism only emerges in 1885, Jackson traces the development of earlier related movements which subsequently provided a secure foundation for unionism. He identifies the Irish Tory party, the Church of Ireland and the Orange Order as the key building blocks for unionism. The Conservatives in Ireland had led the resistance to O'Connellism. Jackson demonstrates that the electoral progress achieved by O'Connell had to be challenged, and he chronicles the meticulous organisation undertaken by his Protestant opponents, which subsequently formed a basis for the advance of Irish Toryism. He describes how Irish Toryism cooperated with the Orange Order to broaden its appeal, though the relationship was often difficult. Indeed, in developing its strength the Irish Tories copied many of the tactics which had proved successful for O'Connell, leaving Jackson to conclude that O'Connell 'proved to be not so much the assassin of Irish Toryism as its tutor'. Jackson attributes the Tory party's dramatic electoral successes in the middle of the century to the shock administered earlier by O'Connell, as the party's organisation was 'created, modified and re-created with a scientific precision and an evangelical enthusiasm'. While he claims that O'Connell inadvertently contributed to the development of a Protestant political consciousness, this was undoubtedly strengthened by the Tory party's bonding with the Orange Order. A crucial figure here was Reverend Henry Cooke, who, Jackson states, helped to create 'a broader Protestant political identity' which, ultimately, helped to prepare the ground for an alliance between Anglicans and Presbyterians in Ulster. Gladstone's 1869 Irish Church Act also played its part in helping to remove denominational differences between Protestants, and, as Jackson records, the earlier evangelical revival of the mid-nineteenth century provided the 'political cement' for Irish Protestantism. Brian Walker, *Ulster Politics: The Formative Years 1868–86* (Belfast, 1989), stresses the importance of Tim Healy's by-election victory in North Monaghan in July 1883. Healy's claim that the nationalist 'invasion' of Ulster had begun really concentrated Protestant minds and proved to be the catalyst in the formation of Ulster unionism. Walker also points out that the franchise extension in 1884 and the subsequent redistribution of seats were pivotal in the development of nationalism and unionism, and he argues that these changes reinforced the existing sectarian divisions in Ulster politics. Eventually, this unionist-nationalist conflict was to lead to partition, though Walker thinks that this division was not inevitable.

More recently, John Bew, *The Glory of Being Britons: Civic Unionism in Nineteenth-Century Belfast* (Dublin, 2008), has examined the development of unionism in the north. He contends that the Napoleonic Wars, the 1832 Great Reform Act and the industrialisation of Britain made more impact on the formation of a 'unionist world-view' than anything connected to an Ulster Scots mentality. Before the 1880s unionism could not be considered as a party political label, but there was an important 'interaction of opinion, ideas and individuals' between Ulster and mainland Britain. In Bew's opinion, moreover, Belfast in the nineteenth century was characterised by a pattern of bourgeois dominance which mirrored developments in Liverpool, Manchester and Glasgow. Bew rejects the view that unionism was defined by its rejection of nationalism, as he cites the positive aspects of a self-confident civic unionism which was interested in economic growth, parliamentary reform, industrial invention and social improvement. These 'unionists' built 'an intellectual, emotional and strategic political bridge' between Britain and Ireland. For Bew, this development took shape in the form of an emerging progressive Conservative grouping in the north with the Conservative MP, James Emerson Tennent very much to the fore. This new group was uncomfortable with pro-Orange, traditional Irish Toryism, and it tended to reflect the progressive values of Peelite Conservatism. Bew concludes that the key to understanding unionism is 'the depth of Ulster's engagement with the British political nation' and its genuine attachment to

British national identity.

Jackson also considers unionism at the close of the century in two earlier works, *Colonel Edward Saunderson: Land and Loyalty in Victorian Ireland* (Oxford, 1995) and *The Ulster Party: Irish Unionists in the House of Commons 1884–1911* (Oxford, 1989). He demonstrates the prominent role played by members of the gentry class in the early Unionist party, arguing that the defence of landlordism was at the heart of emerging unionism. Indeed, Jackson states that it was the challenges faced by Irish landlords that helped to mould unionism, while the class's steady social and economic retreat 'profoundly affected the structure and direction of the movement'. Individual leaders such as Saunderson were appalled that Westminster would consider granting power to the agrarian radicals in the IPP, and early unionism emphasised the importance of the maintenance of law and order. Gradually, as Jackson acknowledges, this landed leadership conceded ground to a more belligerent Ulster bourgeoisie, as the process of 'Ulsterisation' got underway. Nevertheless, Jackson emphatically rejects the earlier argument advanced by Peter Gibbon, *The Origins of Ulster Unionism* (Manchester, 1985), which contended that the Ulster bourgeoisie had assumed the leadership of northern unionism by the time of the 1893 Home Rule Bill. Jackson also stresses that in the period from 1885–1900, unionism was a genuinely Irish movement, and its leader, Edward Saunderson, was an Irish, rather than an Ulster, Unionist. Indeed, what made unionism such a formidable force at the end of the nineteenth century was the effective coalition of Irish landed and Ulster business interests. However, as Jackson notes, Saunderson viewed Ulster Protestantism as the best defence against aggressive agrarian agitation. He was a key influence on Churchill's visit in February 1886, though Jackson demonstrates that it was his lack of confidence in the Tory party that led to his campaign for the formation of an independent Irish Unionist party at Westminster. Significantly, Jackson contends that Saunderson felt 'no unequivocal sense of Britishness' and that his loyalty to the United Kingdom was dependent on the Westminster government continuing to maintain the constitutional status quo and offer an effective defence of Protestant interests. In examining the class tensions within unionism, which surfaced following the defeat of the 1893 Home Rule Bill, Jackson unveils Saunderson's deep suspicion of the liberal agenda advanced by Russell and Plunkett, leaving him to comment that 'by 1900 it was becoming clear that Saunderson was merely the captain of a conservative fragment of Unionism'.

On the issue of the links between pro-Union supporters in Ireland and Britain, Jackson argues that fighting Home Rule in 1886 and 1893 strengthened the bonds between Irish and British Unionists. While many of the Irish Unionist MPs at Westminster were effective debaters, they were not, in the main, interested in British affairs. Moreover, outside these crisis points, Jackson notes that Conservatives showed little real concern for Ireland. Patrick Buckland, *Irish Unionism I: The Anglo-Irish and the new Ireland 1885–1922* (Dublin, 1973), emphasises the importance of the links between southern unionism and British Conservatism, particularly the family ties that had been established through marriage. Buckland also highlights the class consciousness at the heart of southern unionism, illustrating the fears that a Home Rule parliament would be dominated by lower class Catholics, whose political failings and lack of ability might bankrupt the landed gentry. In his analysis of the relationship between Unionists in the north and south, Buckland argues that from the early 1890s Ulstermen were becoming increasingly more exclusive and independent. He states that once Ulster Unionists had woken up to the threat of Home Rule, they preferred to fight on their own. To overcome their electoral weakness, Buckland describes how southern Unionists used their money to target marginal seats in Britain in 1886 and 1893, adding that while they held only the two Trinity seats in the south in 1886, there were seventeen southern Unionists representing British constituencies.

The increased focus on Irish unionism during the last two decades, led by Jackson's work, has produced some of the best 'revisionist' history, as historians have looked beyond simple explanations of the two states established in 1920–22. Unionism during the nineteenth century covered a broad spectrum of opinion, and recent historiography has placed a much greater focus on the understanding of liberal unionism. One such example is Matthew Potter, *Willam Monsell of Tervoe 1812–1894: Catholic Unionist, Anglo-Irishman* (Dublin, 2009), which examines support for the Union among members of the Catholic gentry like Monsell. Such men, some of whom were educated in England, were sincere in their belief that a legislative union provided the best form of government for Ireland. While Monsell was clearly a liberal unionist, he regarded the Land League as a socialist movement and was convinced that Home Rule would destroy Ireland's social system. He and other members of the Catholic gentry believed that 'progress and civilisation' depended on the maintenance of social ranks, and they deplored violence and revolution. Potter shares the argument expressed by Linda Colley, *Britons: Forging the Nation 1707–1837* (New Haven, 1992), which suggests that a British nation was constructed between these dates from the four component countries of the United Kingdom – England, Scotland, Wales and Ireland – which made it possible for elites to have dual nationality. It was also true, however, that Protestantism was at the heart of this identity, which had been invented in the eighteenth century, and Britain was envisaged as an island outpost besieged by continental Catholicism.

# Index of historians

# General index

**Colourpoint**
Educational

# Also available:

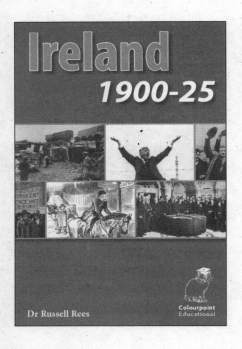

## Ireland 1900-25
ISBN: 978 1 906578 00 8
Price: £14.00
Author: Dr Russell Rees

Contact Colourpoint Educational at:

**Tel: 028 9182 6339  Fax: 028 9182 1900**

**Web: www.colourpointeducational.com**

**Colourpoint Books, Colourpoint House, Jubilee Business Park, 21 Jubilee Road, Newtownards, Co Down, BT23 4YH**

All orders to MiMO Distribution:

**Tel: 028 9182 0505**

**E-mail: sales@mimodistribution.co.uk**